IS MORMONISM NOW CHRISTIAN?

Is Mormonism Now Christian?

STEVEN A. CRANE

WIPF & STOCK · Eugene, Oregon

IS MORMONISM NOW CHRISTIAN?

Wipf & Stock
An Imprint of Wipf and Stock Publishers
199 W. 8th Ave., Suite 3
Eugene, OR 97401

www.wipfandstock.com

ISBN: 978-1-60899-251-5

Manufactured in the U.S.A.

Contents

Introduction

SEVERAL YEARS ago, a young couple sat in my office seeking premarital counseling. They were bright, enthusiastic, well-groomed, well-educated, and both had assured me that they were Christian believers actively involved in their respective churches. As I worked my way through my customary premarital counseling material, however, I began to suspect that while the young man had likely grown-up in an evangelical home, the young woman must have been raised in the Church of Jesus Christ of Latter-day Saints (LDS). After more discussion, their comments continued to confirm my suspicions that she was indeed, Mormon.[1] When I was sure about my conclusions, I finally asked this simple question: "Have you considered the ramifications of being unequally yoked?" This young couple looked at me with shocked expressions on their faces. While they didn't know precisely where to find this teaching (2 Corinthians 6:14), both knew I was referencing Scripture. Their surprise came not from my mention of this biblical verse, but from my assertion that this passage somehow applied to them! "We're both Christians," was their response.

In turn, I too, was shocked! They were well aware of each other's spiritual background—did they not realize the significant differences between their faiths? Would their families not also object to this marriage? What about the LDS leaders from her church? Would they condone such a union? These and other questions ran through my mind.

---

1. While LDS Church authorities have sometimes suggested moving away from the term "Mormon" in reference to its followers, it is by far the most recognized reference and will commonly be used in this book.

Mormonism has taught since its inception that all the creeds of Christianity were an abomination and all other churches were corrupt (Pearl of Great Price, Joseph Smith 1:19). Joseph Smith was told not to join with any of them, but to help lead in what would be a restoration of the true church. In the same way, Christianity has never accepted the Mormon church among their ranks, considering them teachers of a different gospel (Galatians 1:6).

As I ministered in the Northwest, the above encounter became just one of many such episodes. I have since met people from both religious faiths who seem willing to blur the lines. To some extent this has always been true among the less informed, but the increasing desire of the Mormon church itself to be considered and ranked among Christian churches,[2] and the willingness of some within the realms of conservative Christianity to classify Mormons as Christians is significant.[3] This new ecumenical spirit of openness suggests to some that the doctrinal distance between these two groups is shrinking. Are the two sides actually moving closer together? Is there significant change within the ranks of Mormonism? If so, is the change widespread? Does this new direction reflect the leadership of the Mormon church, or is it simply the belief of a few? Worse yet, is it a deceptive media ploy on behalf of the Church of Jesus Christ of Latter-day Saints (LDS) to appear to be something it is not?[4]

---

2. This desire to be known as Christian is apparent in many newly released articles and publications. Take for example, *The Idaho Statesman*, February 24, 2001. "In a new move to identify their faith as Christians, leaders of the Church of Jesus Christ of Latter-day Saints will soon issue a formal statement dropping the terms 'LDS Church' and 'LDS' as shorthand names . . . from now on the preferred shorthand or second reference should be simply 'the church' or 'the Church of Jesus Christ' . . . the church has taken a series of steps to re-emphasize its Christian roots."

3. Former President Jimmy Carter has declared Mormons to be Christians. *Deseret News*, Salt Lake City, November 15, 1997. Other Christians have embraced similar sentiments in varying degrees, including Richard J. Mouw, president of Christian philosophy at Fuller Theological Seminary in Pasadena, California.

4. The Mormon Church has mounted an aggressive public relations cam-

Christian churches, especially in the West, must constantly face the pressure of ministering in a Latter-day Saint environment. The high density Mormon population creates a unique dynamic that necessitates the ability to explain the distinctives of the Christian faith, defend the accuracy of the Bible, and preach an accurate reflection of Christ to people influenced by this theology. For this reason it is necessary to wrestle with current trends in Mormon doctrine and how they relate to Christianity.

Section One of this book will closely examine recent dialogues (both written and verbal) between leaders of the evangelical community and the Mormon faith, to determine whether or not the gap is shrinking between the two movements, or if the apparent shift is due to the use of ambiguous terminology. We will proceed by critiquing the major players and their significant works. These works include: Craig Blomberg and Steven Robinson's book, *How Wide the Divide? A Mormon and Evangelical in Conversation*;[5] Steven Robinson's book, *Are Mormons Christians?*;[6] Robert Millet's recent offering, *A Different Jesus? The Christ of the Latter-day Saints*;[7] and dialogues entitled, "Conversations: A Mormon and Evangelical in Conversation." These dialogues between Greg Johnson and LDS writer Robert Millet have been held across the nation—one of which was held at Eagle Christian Church, where I minister. We need to address this issue of: "What (if anything) has changed" in Mormonism.

In Section Two, we will conduct a theological review covering the following issues: the scriptural rationale for a Christian to

paign. They flood local markets with well-designed, appealing television commercials with an offer of a free Book of Mormon, or more recently, a King James Bible. Mormonism portrays itself as a mainstream Christian movement.

5. Blomberg, Craig L., and Stephen E. Robinson. *How Wide the Divide? A Mormon and an Evangelical in Conversation.* Downers Grove, Illinois: InterVarsity Press, 1997.

6. Robinson, Stephen E. *Are Mormons Christians?* Salt Lake City: Bookcraft, 1991.

7. Millet, Robert L. *A Different Jesus? The Christ of the Latter-day Saints.* Grand Rapids: Eerdmans, 2005.

undergo such a project of examining Christianity and Mormonism; a comparison between the stated beliefs of the Christian and the Mormon church; and an evaluation of whether or not (if there are significant differences) Mormons should be classified as Christian.

My hope is to communicate in a clear, effective, and non-combative way the differences between Christianity and Mormonism. My goal is that this will be a valuable resource for preachers (and others) in the local churches in the greater Northwest and beyond. I will also include insights into how best to continue dialogues between Christians and Mormons without compromising foundational beliefs.

PART ONE

Is Mormonism Changing?
Current Dialogues Between Christians and Mormons

"I believe that every faith I have encountered draws its adherents closer to God. And in every faith I have come to know, there are features I wish were my own . . . It's important to recognize that while differences in theology exist between the churches in America, we share a common creed of moral convictions."[1]

—Mitt Romney

WALLACE: "Is a Mormon a true Christian?"

OSTEEN: "Well, in my mind they are. Mitt Romney has said that he believes in Christ as his savior, and that's what I believe."[2]

—Chris Wallace and Joel Osteen

This section will closely examine recent dialogues (both written and verbal) between leaders of the evangelical community and the Mormon faith, to determine whether or not the gap is shrinking between the two movements, or if the apparent shift is due to the use of ambiguous terminology.

---

1. Mitt Romney's speech as recorded by The Associated Press, December 6, 2007.

2. News Brief: "Joel Osteen, Interviewed by Chris Wallace of Fox News," December 23, 2007.

1

Hopeful, but Not Convinced

"Could it be that I was face to face with a Christian? Perhaps. Nonetheless, I continued my checklist."[1]

—Max Lucado

As I grew up in Salt Lake City, our family enjoyed taking friends and relatives to the Temple Square downtown to let them experience first-hand the flavor of Mormonism. It always proved to be an eye-opener for visitors as they were exposed to the teachings of Joseph Smith and Brigham Young, many for the first time. They would walk through what we called "the Hall of Fame," see pictures of Mormon prophets, and hear their history. They would be exposed to stories of the beginnings of Mormonism in Palmyra, New York, and finally to Joseph Smith and his first vision.

It was during this portion of the tour that visitors would learn the foundational beliefs of Mormonism. As they listened to the unfolding of the first vision, they would discern that Joseph Smith was told that all Christian sects were an abomination and that he should join none of them. They would hear how the Mormon church claimed to be the one and only true church, severing Mormonism from all who practice Christianity.

Much has changed since those days including the temple tour. Most of the distinctive terminology of Mormonism has been erased in favor of a more "mainstream" approach. The hall of fame is no longer available to tourists. The woodland scene of Joseph

1. Lucado, *A Gentle Thunder: Hearing God Through the Storm*, 139.

Smith prayerfully retrieving the golden tablets has been removed and is now a counseling center. Gone is their vocabulary of being the one and only true church. Even the title of the Book of Mormon has undergone a change with the phrase, "Another Testament of Jesus Christ" being added in 1982. From the perspective of a casual observer, there appeared either a move toward evangelical Christianity, or at least a deliberate attempt to appear more mainstream.[2] I questioned what I saw happening, but for several years, did little to confirm or deny my suspected beliefs—until I came in contact with Robert Millet and Greg Johnson.[3]

Dr. Robert Millet (a Mormon) and Greg Johnson (an evangelical minister)[4] have hosted dialogues on the similarities and differences between their respective faiths.[5] If a person wants to be current on the discussions that are happening between Mormonism and evangelical Christianity, these are the key players.

Robert Millet and Greg Johnson—A Mormon and an Evangelical Christian in Conversation

My first experience with inter-faith dialogues was in March 2004, when Robert Millet and Greg Johnson held their "In Conversation"[6]

---

2. In the early 1990s, even the official logo of the church was altered, making the name "Jesus Christ" three times larger than the rest of the title.

3. Jon Strain of Search Ministries first introduced me to Greg Johnson at a minister's meeting and later arranged for me to meet Bob Millet.

4. Robert Millet is the Professor of Religious Understanding at Brigham Young University. He has served at BYU for over twenty-three years and is the author of over fifty LDS books. Greg Johnson is a former Mormon and ordained Baptist pastor. He is the founder and Director of *Standing Together* and was the catalyst in bringing together a Mormon and an Evangelical scholar to write a landmark book, *How Wide the Divide: A Mormon & Evangelical in Conversation*.

5. I have been privileged to be a witness to these dialogues and have even hosted one at Eagle Christian Church, where I minister. It is these discussions, in part, which have given rise to the formulation of this book.

6. Robert Millet and Greg Johnson, "A Mormon & Evangelical Christian in Conversation: Truth Matters, People Matter, Relationships Matter, Lunch

in Boise, Idaho. I was immediately impressed with the tone and tenor of their conversations.[7] These dialogues were friendly, interactive discussions with in-depth give-and-take on various theological topics. The conversations were engaging and yet conducted in such a manner as to earn the reputation of being done with "convicted civility"—a term coined by Richard Mouw[8] to describe two people who own their convictions, but share their disagreements in a civil way. While impressed with the tone of these discussions, my overall reaction was one of intrigue.

The first dialogue was entitled "Truth matters, People matter, Relationships matter, Lunch matters." The basic premise was that in order for one person to influence another, they must first learn to trust, listen, and care about what the other person is saying. Dr. Millet and Greg Johnson have done just that—built a solid relationship and earned the right to speak freely to one another. Their friendship enables them to discuss theology in a manner in which both parties can learn and dialogue without fear of compromise. Those present at this discussion benefitted from the friendship and respect they share.

As I listened to these men communicate, I was amazed at what was said. I heard theological language from Dr. Millet that, frankly, I had never heard uttered by a Mormon. I honestly didn't know what to do with it. Dr. Millet talked about God, Jesus, and even grace in language I would expect from an evangelical. Having grown up in Salt Lake City, and having experienced the changes in the Temple tour, this new dialogue heightened the questions which had already haunted me. Was the Church of Jesus Christ of Latter-day Saints changing? Or was this simply a media ploy? Specifically, I wanted to know: "Does Robert Millet truly believe

---

Matters." Boise, Idaho: Search Ministries, 2004.

7. Three dialogues have been held in Boise and repeated across the United States. These dialogues are available on DVD.

8. Richard Mouw is president of Fuller Theological Seminary in Pasadena, California.

what he is saying?" If so, "Does Robert Millet merely speak for himself, or is this representative of all of Mormonism?"

Dr. Millet addressed this in the dialogue.

> People have come up to me and told me, "What you are saying is not what my Mormon neighbor says!" I simply reply, "I can't speak for what your neighbor said, I wasn't there, but I do believe I speak on behalf of what the Mormon church teaches or at least what it is supposed to teach."[9]

Later, I had the opportunity to speak directly with Dr. Millet. He explained to me that the LDS Church has undergone a doctrinal refinement. "This is not a change in Mormon theology, but a clarifying and refocusing on redemptive theology, based on Ezra Taft Benson's[10] instructions to 'get back to the Book of Mormon.'"

Could it be that Mormonism was shifting? After this dialogue I was cautiously optimistic that the Church of Jesus Christ of Latter-day Saints was moving toward mainstream Christianity. I began praying in earnest that something would happen within the LDS Church similar to what happened with the World-Wide Church of God.

Several months later my hopes were heightened as Dr. Ravi Zacharias, through the ministries of *Standing Together*, was invited to speak at the Mormon Tabernacle in Salt Lake City in November of 2004. This marked the first time since Dwight L. Moody, that a non-Mormon was permitted to speak in this facility. I took this to be yet another sign of a potential change within Mormonism. With excitement, I traveled to Utah to hear Dr. Zacharias give a message on the deity of Christ. This event, with this man, in this unique forum (the Mormon Tabernacle) certainly brought with it a feeling of expectation.[11] Strangely absent, however, were the white shirts

---

9. Millet, *Truth Matters*, March, 2004.

10. Ezra Taft Benson was the thirteenth Prophet of the LDS Church, serving for eight and a half years.

11. Dr. Zacharias is the new editor of Walter Martin's classic *The Kingdom of the Cults*. What an interesting situation to have him speak at the Mormon Tabernacle.

and ties that I expected to see in this particular venue. The audience was predominately filled with evangelical Christians.

After this weekend trip, I was more determined than ever to find out to what extent, if any, the Mormon church had moved from historical Mormonism to a more mainstream approach.

The second conversation with Dr. Millet and Greg Johnson was entitled "The First Vision of Joseph Smith."[12] The speakers explored the question, "Did God appear in a vision to Joseph Smith and give him authority to restore the one true Church on the face of the earth?"[13] While Dr. Millet mourned the fact that few evangelicals regard Mormons as Christians, Greg Johnson reminded him that it was Joseph Smith and his first vision that created the dividing line.[14] Dr. Millet tried to soften the words of the Prophet (that all other churches were an abomination) by quoting a passage out of the Doctrine and Covenants. However, very little was discussed that evening to help answer my questions as to whether or not Mormonism had set out in a new direction.

The third and most interesting discussion between Dr. Millet and Greg Johnson was entitled, "The Nature of Jesus Christ."[15] Like previous conversations, I approached this meeting with excitement and anticipation, but my attitude soon changed from intrigue to concern. I discovered what I was hearing was not all that new.

---

12. Millet, *The First Vision of Joseph Smith*, March 4, 2005.

13. The First Vision is significant to a Mormon for a number of reasons. First, Latter-day Saints have used this event to support the notion that God the Father and Jesus Christ are two separate and distinct personages and two distinct and separate gods. Second, it gives Mormonism justification to believe Christianity had fallen into complete apostasy and needed restoration.

14. In his first vision, Joseph Smith was told that corruption had taken hold of the church and ultimately destroyed the succession of Jesus' apostles. He was told that God had rejected all other churches, not to join any other church, and that the true church would be reestablish on earth. The true church supposedly restored the priesthood and the authority to baptize. See the Pearl of Great Price 1:5–19 for details.

15. Millet, *The Nature of Jesus Christ*, February 15, 2006.

From the outset of the meeting, Dr. Millet let it be known that he felt we concentrate far too much on our differences and too little on our similarities. "God will not be upset if we have similarities,"[16] he said. I greatly appreciated his effort to "stand together," but also recognized that it is our distinctives that make us different.

Dr. Millet and Greg Johnson began the discussion about Christ with a checklist of commonalities between Mormonism and Christianity. The list included: the dual nature of Jesus; the virgin birth of Christ; that Jesus was fully human and underwent temptation; that while tempted he remained sinless; that he died, was buried and physically rose from the dead—each obviously a key issue when it comes to the nature of Christ. If the LDS church believed these things as stated, there was no doubt that Mormonism had taken a dramatic shift toward evangelical Christianity!

I could barely contain myself. If this was true, we were witnessing a historic event. Still, I wanted to ask, "Are these really views both faiths hold? Are these areas in which we both agree?" Several times as the conversation progressed, I wanted to stop the dialogue and simply respond, "Not so quickly. If what you are saying is accurate, things have certainly changed within Mormonism."[17]

As the evening went on, I began to realize that the perceived similarities were due only to a difference in definitions. Dr. Millet and Greg Johnson were using identical words, but the words had very different connotations. By listening carefully, one by one, clear distinctions came to light. One such moment came when Dr. Millet affirmed,

> I believe in the historical Jesus. Do you believe my Jesus was born in Philadelphia? Do you think my Jesus grew up in Detroit? Do you think we believe Jesus died of asphyxiation? Of course not! We believe in the Christ of the New Testament. We believe that Christ is literally the Son of God.[18]

---

16. Ibid.

17. Remember, this dialogue took place at the church where I minister.

18. Millet, *The Nature of Jesus Christ*, February 15, 2006.

At this point, Greg Johnson chimed in, "The literal Son of God?"

Dr. Millet responded, "Yes. Ezra Taft Benson used the word sired, although I don't know exactly what that means."

"So you believe that Jesus is the physical son of God?" Johnson asked.

"Yes, evangelicals believe that Jesus is the son of God in some metaphysical sense. We believe that Jesus is the literal, physical and spiritual Son of God."[19] Millet also acknowledged that the Mormon God has a physical body.[20]

While believing in a Jesus who lived in Nazareth, born in Bethlehem, the Mormon Jesus was described as being the literal offspring of the God Elohim who had a physical body. While this is in keeping with historical Mormonism, it is a dramatic departure from conservative Christianity![21]

The differences didn't end there. When asked if the Mormons believe that Jesus had been God for all eternity, Dr. Millet replied, "Yes."

Greg Johnson followed up with this question: "So do you believe that Jesus has always been God?"

At this point we heard an interesting definition of "eternal." Dr. Millet suggested that while Mormons believe that Jesus has been God for eternity, there was a time before eternity, when Jesus wasn't God. According to Dr. Millet, eternity only refers to a "long period of time." In other words, Jesus hasn't always been God, only god for a long time. Here is the explanation he gave:

---

19. Ibid.

20. Reconcile that with the biblical teaching that God is omnipresent or passages like John 4:24 which tells us that "God is spirit."

21. Some might argue that the use of "conservative Christian" or "evangelical" is too vague or imprecise and would prefer the use of words like "orthodox," "historic," or even "creedal" Christianity. The LDS church, however, argues that it was the early church creeds that corrupted the church, and to use such words is ineffective.

> Latter-day Saints do believe that Christ is the Spirit son, the firstborn spirit son of God. What we do not know, really, is how long a time there was until he was, what we would call God. We don't know much about that really. I do know there was an eternity of time that he was God and that is why he is called Eternal God.[22]

While Latter-day Saints may believe in the "historical Jesus,"[23] the Jesus of Mormonism certainly is not the same "theological Jesus"[24] as that of evangelicals. This redefinition of eternity has long-lasting ramifications. If eternity only means a long time, are we to assume heaven is only going to last a long time as well?[25] Has God only been god for a long time? The definition of words is critical. We cannot honestly speak of believing in the same eternality of Christ while using different definitions of the word eternal. When referring to Jesus, evangelical Christianity believes that eternal means forever.

I found two other topics revealing. The first had to deal with classifying Mormons as Christians. Dr. Millet admitted, "I've been asked hundreds of times if Mormons are Christians, of course they are." He then explained that when he asks most Christians why they don't classify Mormons as Christians, they typically respond: "Because we don't know what to do with you—you're not Catholic and you are not Protestant. You don't fall into the historic line of Christian Churches." He then defended the "historic tradition" of Mormonism.

> Mormons are Christians because of the historic line of church-es. What were the Mormons like before [they were Mormons]? They were Christian. They were Protestant. They didn't just appear! They didn't come out of nowhere. They were Baptists. They were Methodists. That means—their historic line was the

---

22. Millet, *The Nature of Jesus Christ*, February 15, 2006.

23. "Historical" in the sense that they believe that Jesus was truly a man who lived in the first century.

24. Their Jesus is different from the Jesus the Bible describes in John 1:1–15.

25. The same word is used in the phrase "eternal life."

same as Greg's historic line. Mormons came from the same
historic tradition, from a Protestant tradition.[26]

Dr. Millet's argument is simple, but flawed. He suggests
that although Mormonism is a late arrival on the scene, it had its
roots in historic Christianity. Since its people came out of various Christian churches, he argues that they should, therefore, be
considered Christian. This is faulty thinking. The Jehovah's
Witnesses, Jim Jones, and David Koresh all had ties to conservative Christianity—should we consider them "mainstream" as well?
It is not your historic ties that make you Christian, but what you
believe.

The most important part of the dialogue came midway
through the discussion. Dr. Millet made the comment: "You have
had two thousand years to work out your theology, we've only been
at this for 175 years."[27] He talked about the process of doctrinal
refinement. While Christianity has been around for two thousand
years, and there have been disagreements, Christianity has never
"switched" directions or "changed" what it believes. Our foundation has remained steadfast, unchanged, and unmoveable. We base
our faith on the person of Jesus Christ and the authority of God's
word: infallible, unaltered, steadfast and true. 2 Peter 1:16ff[28] says:

> We did not follow cleverly invented stories when we told
> you about the power and coming of our Lord Jesus Christ,
> but we were eyewitnesses of his majesty . . . and we have the
> word of the prophets made certain, and you will do well to
> pay attention to it . . . above all, you must understand that
> no prophecy of Scripture came about by the prophet's own
> interpretation. For prophecy never had its origin in the will of
> man, but men spoke from God as they were carried along by
> the Holy Spirit.

---

26. Millet, *The Nature of Jesus Christ*, February 15, 2006.

27. Ibid.

28. All Scripture has been quoted from the New International Version of
the Bible (NIV).

In contrast, Dr. Millet repeatedly said, "Don't hold us responsible for everything that some Mormon has said in the last 175 years." He went on to say:

> We are not a static unit . . . we are not sitting still . . . We have undergone in the last fifty years, in the last thirty years, a different emphasis on redemptive doctrines—development. Should that bother someone? Not if you believe you are a living church. And part of a living church is bringing change and understanding and clarity. If you want to know what [current] Latter-day Saints believe, pay attention to what [current] Saints are saying. Judge the church by the church today.[29]

Dr. Millet teased, "Don't hold us accountable for everything we've said and we won't hold you accountable for everything you've said." I would respond, "Please do hold me accountable for every word I've said. Judge everything by the sure and steadfast standard of the word of God." We need to judge the church leaders who have gone before us (Luther, Wesley, Calvin) by the sure standard of God's word. We should, and must, hold others accountable as well as be held accountable by others.

Dr. Millet continued:

> We love, we honor, we revere, we respect our prophet leaders of the past, but we do not believe in the infallibility of the Apostles and Prophets. Peter wasn't infallible. Paul wasn't infallible. David O. McKay[30] said, "when God makes a prophet he doesn't unmake the man."[31]

Dr. Millet doesn't believe the prophets, past or present, to be infallible. Here we find the crux of the issue. Mormonism does not believe that the Bible is the infallible word of God. Mormonism does not believe that their Prophets (and therefore their own teachings) are infallible, therefore the purpose of the current Prophet

---

29. Millet, *The Nature of Jesus Christ*, February 15, 2006.

30. David O. McKay was the ninth LDS Prophet, serving from 1951–1970.

31. Millet, *The Nature of Jesus Christ*, February 15, 2006.

and the LDS church organization is to keep the church moving in the right direction.

Dr. Millet said:

> The reason we study the Bible, the reason we study scriptures and past Prophets is so we can see how they communicated with God and so we can become better able to hear him ourselves.[32]

According to Dr. Millet, Mormonism can and does change. After this dialogue, I began to have my doubts as to whether it was moving in the direction of evangelical Christianity. This raised yet another question in my mind, "If the church can change, and maybe even move in the direction of conservative Christianity, what prevents it from moving away as well?"[33]

Dr. Millet made one more statement during the third conversation to which I was able to give a response. He asked: "Why don't Christians trust us?" That evening, I simply responded that we don't know if what is being said is real, or simply a media ploy on behalf of the Mormon church to appear mainstream Christian. We cannot tell whether Bob Millet is representative of all of Mormonism or just an aberration. If we can only judge Mormon doctrine based on the standard works of Mormonism, or by an official proclamation of the leadership of the LDS Church (as Dr. Millet suggests), we have no other option available to us but skepticism until the LDS leadership takes an official position and clarifies these issues.

That third dialogue caused quite a stir at our church. People did not know quite how to respond. Some were upset merely by listening to the dialogue. Others were disturbed because no clear objectives were met. Others were encouraged by seeing people disagree in a congenial manner. Personally, I think these dialogues served a good purpose. My desire is that these dialogues will continue in the future and I might be able to contribute to them.

---

32. Ibid.

33. I asked Dr. Millet about what prevents the church from changing in the wrong direction to which he responded, "True doctrine has staying power."

When asked after the third dialogue if I thought Mormonism was changing, I responded, that "I'm hopeful, but not convinced." While I would and do regard some within the Mormon church to be Christian, Mormonism itself still differs radically on many foundational points from conservative Christianity. As for Bob Millet, I would never hesitate to question his love, loyalty, and sincerity, and do wish to grant him the title of friend.

After these dialogues I was more determined than ever to seek out current Mormon material to determine the distance between these two faiths. Outside of the dialogues between Dr. Millet and Greg Johnson, there are three landmark books that shed light on our particular topic. We will now turn our attention to these works.

2

Of Course, We're Christians

"If the term Christian is understood to mean someone who believes that Jesus is the Christ, the Son of God and the Savior of the world, and who believes that the Old and New Testaments contain his teachings, then the Mormons are Christians."[1]

—Stephen E. Robinson

In 1991, Stephen E. Robinson authored a book entitled, *Are Mormons Christians?* This was the first book published by a Mormon author whose sole and primary purpose was to establish Mormonism squarely within the boundaries of mainstream Christianity. As noted earlier, the desire to be associated with other mainstream Christian churches does represent a change in LDS thought.

In his book, Robinson examines and refutes what he believes to be the six most frequently used arguments used to exclude the Latter-day Saints from the family of "Christian" churches. He categorizes these arguments as:

> (1) exclusion by definition; (2) exclusion by misrepresentation; (3) exclusion by name-calling (the ad hominem exclusion); (4) the historical or traditional exclusion; (5) the canonical or biblical exclusion; and, (6) the doctrinal exclusion.[2]

---

1. Robinson, *Are Mormons Christians?*, 4.

2. Ibid., ix. While I will not address all of these issues, I will address the main underlying arguments.

Robinson wants his readers to conclude that Mormonism has been misunderstood and unfairly ostracized. While he admits that significant differences do exist between the Church of Jesus Christ of Latter-day Saints and evangelical Christianity, he maintains that these differences do not warrant sufficient cause to exclude Mormonism from the ranks of orthodox Christianity. He even suggests that if the same arguments used against the LDS were applied to the first century church, they too, would not be considered Christian.[3]

To the casual, uninformed reader, several of Robinson's arguments might hold sway. To the critical eye, however, Robinson's arguments are severely flawed. One example can be found in Robinson's definition of Christianity. He argues that Mormons suffer from exclusion by definition—stacking the deck against Mormonism by selecting too narrow a definition.

To remedy this problem, Robinson proposes a very broad definition of Christianity straight from his Webster's Dictionary. A Christian is:

> One who believes or professes or is assumed to believe in Jesus Christ and the truth taught by him: an adherent of Christianity: one who has accepted the Christian religious and moral principles of life: one who has faith in and has pledged allegiance to God thought of as revealed in Christ . . . a member of a church or group professing Christian doctrine or belief.[4]

Notice some of the stated assumptions in his proposed definition and ask if this is how one should determine an adherent to Christianity. Should a "Christian" be classified as one who is "assumed to believe in Jesus Christ?" Should a person be included among the ranks of Christianity because they have merely "accepted the Christian religious and moral principles of life?" Is one deemed "Christian" simply because he is "a member of a church professing Christian doctrine or belief?"

---

3. Ibid., 29.

4. Ibid., 1.

Such a broad and inclusive definition might succeed in including the LDS faith as Christian,[5] but would also legitimize many other faiths as well. Don't Muslims hold, to some extent, a belief in Jesus Christ? Don't many atheists and agnostics accept some of the moral principles of Christianity? Isn't this dictionary type of definition used to classify the United States as a Christian nation? Do we really want to use a Webster's dictionary definition to determine someone's inclusion into Christianity? Robinson's definition is too broad for any useful discussion on this topic.

Actually, Robinson's argument is a little ironic. Robinson's premise is that Christian sects knowingly and deliberately choose overly-precise definitions to exclude Mormons from their ranks. This, he claims, is exclusion by definition. Instead, Robinson chooses the opposite approach of inclusion by definition—using a definition so broad as to include most everyone within the ranks of Christianity. Most of Robinson's six arguments adopt a similar practice of redefining words or practices to make room for Mormonism within Christianity.

Another problem stems from what Robinson labels, "the exclusion by misrepresentation"—anti-Mormons have distorted Mormon teaching and for this reason, Mormons have been excluded. Robinson suggests that if LDS theology was properly understood, Christians would include Mormons within their fellowship.

> When non-Mormons attempt to impose doctrines on the Latter-day Saints or interpret them for us, the resulting fictions generally fall into one of three categories: outright fabrications, distortions of genuine LDS doctrines into unrecognizable forms, or the representation of anomalies within the LDS tradition as mainline or official LDS teaching.[6]

Robinson insists that we let him define what he does and does not believe and then judge whether Mormonism is Christian.

---

5. One could also argue that if you exegete Robinson's own definition, the phrase "believe in Jesus Christ and the truth taught by him," Mormonism would be excluded from the ranks of Christianity.

6. Robinson, *Are Mormons Christians?*, 10.

I have several problems with this approach. First of all, Robinson acknowledges that he does not speak on behalf of the Mormon church. In fact, he makes it clear that he does not speak in any formal capacity. "It should be understood that I do not speak officially for the LDS church or for Brigham Young University. While I believe the opinions expressed here to be soundly based, I alone am responsible for them."[7] Are we to classify the soundness of a religious organization, based on one man's unofficial opinion?

My second reservation stems from the fact that Robinson wants to limit the discussion of Mormon doctrine only to the standard works of the church. By limiting the scope of investigation, he effectively purges the record of some of the historically controversial doctrines of the LDS church. To substantiate this move, he quotes B. H. Roberts:

> The Church has confined the sources of doctrine by which it is willing to be bound before the world to the things that God has revealed, and which the Church has officially accepted, and those alone. These would include the Bible, the Book of Mormon, the Doctrine and Covenants, the Pearl of Great Price; these have been repeatedly accepted and endorsed by the Church in general conference assembled, and are the only sources of absolute appeal for our doctrine.[8]

In this one statement, much within Mormonism is nullified or made irrelevant, including most of the teaching of their Prophets (Joseph Smith, Brigham Young, Lorenzo Snow, David O. McKay, Ezra Taft Benson, Gordon B. Hinckley, etc.),[9] as well as official publications of the LDS church.

It is curious that on such a pertinent matter, (the exclusion of past teachings of Mormonism's own Prophets), Robinson does not quote from a standard work to support his case, but rather from B. H. Roberts. The question needs to be asked, "Who is B. H.

---

7. Ibid., ix.

8. Ibid., 14. Quoting from a sermon of July 10, 1921, delivered in the Salt Lake Tabernacle.

9. These are some of the most often quoted Prophets of Mormonism.

Roberts?" Roberts is a General Authority of the LDS Church. But the above statement makes Roberts' own remarks, non-binding and therefore irrelevant. Robinson clearly acknowledges this when he says, "The General Authorities are not inspired."[10] Does this not demonstrate a certain amount of inconsistency? Robinson makes a binding statement from a source which he deems to be unbinding. Is Robinson suggesting that he can use Mormon material when it benefits his cause, but will not allow others to use the same material if it does not? More importantly, it is puzzling that official authorities of the church and even the Prophets themselves can be deemed unofficial?[11]

Hoping to gloss over this obvious inconsistency, Robinson makes a distinction between receiving inspiration from God and inspiration which is of binding authority. "Latter-day Saints believe that the General Authorities receive inspiration and revelation from God constantly . . . They also believe that individuals within the Church may receive personal revelation, even on doctrinal matters."[12]

Does Robinson really believe that inspiration from God is not necessarily binding? How, then, does a message from God become of binding authority for the LDS church? Robinson answers by saying that material is only binding when it receives approval from the President of the Church and is sustained by a positive vote by the general conference of the Church. "Some things may be correct without being official Church doctrine."[13] Again, I am at a loss at

---

10. Robinson, *Are Mormons Christians?*, 17.

11. This is inconsistent with teachings of the LDS Church. Note the following quote from President Kimball regarding the words of their prophets and church publications. "In addition to these four books of scripture, the inspired words of our living prophets become scripture to us. Their words come to us through conferences, Church publications, and instructions to local priesthood leaders" (*The Teachings of Spencer W. Kimball*, 434).

12. Robinson, *Are Mormons Christians?*, 17.

13. Ibid.

this point. If revelation is true, why shouldn't such information be used in an examination of Mormonism?[14]

Please note that Robinson's argument contains a double standard. Any time a non-Mormon quotes material outside the boundaries of the standard works, it is not official Mormon doctrine and cannot be cited as representative of the church. But this does not limit Mormon authors or Robinson himself from making doctrinal statements about the church, or quoting Mormon material in defense of his position. Robinson quotes from Mormon authors more than two dozen times in this book to convey what he believes to be true Mormon doctrine.[15] Shouldn't non-Mormons have the same right to evaluate this material?

Robinson would have us believe the only avenue by which non-Mormons have successfully excluded the LDS church from within the bounds of Christianity is by quoting obscure sources from the periphery of Mormon thought[16] or by misquoting the standard works. This is not the case. A close examination of non-Mormon authors will show that they quote the very sources Robinson himself quotes.

There can be no doubt that overzealous critics from both sides of the divide have made unwarranted attacks and unfounded

---

14. Bill McKeever writes, "It is irrelevant to say these teachings should not be given serious consideration because they are not in the standard works. Were these leaders teaching truth when they spoke or weren't they? If they were, what does it matter if it is not in the standard works? If they were not teaching truth, why should members be compelled to honor them as godly spiritual guides?" (*Questions to Ask Your Mormon Friend*, 43).

15. For example, Robinson specifically tries to distance himself from the *Journal of Discourses* and yet quotes from it himself. Note also the Preface to the *Journal of Discourses*. "The Journal of Discourses deservedly ranks as one of the standard works of the Church, and every rightminded Saint will certainly welcome with joy every Number as it comes forth from the press as an additional reflector of "the light that shines from Zion's hill."

16. It is interesting to note, that when defining Christian thought, Robinson chooses Robert Tilton and Kenneth Copeland as examples. *Are Mormons Christians?*, 63.

claims against those on the other side. But unwarranted attacks against the "Saints"[17] are not what is creating this divide.

In answering the question, "Are Mormons Christians?" Robinson poses another question to his readers. "Is not the name of our church The Church of *Jesus Christ* of Latter-day Saints? Do we not worship Christ? Is not the Book of Mormon another testament of Jesus Christ?"[18] This same argument has often been encountered by those who have tried to dialogue about this topic with a Mormon. The answer to the first part of this question is, obviously, yes—the LDS name includes the use of Jesus Christ.

However, does the name of an organization or a name on a church validate a church's teaching? Of course not! By that logic, everything inside McDonalds should be classified as a hamburger and everything in my garage is most certainly a car. It is not the name on the door of a church that matters, but the beliefs that are taught and espoused that distinguish a religious body. While the title of an organization might bear the name of Jesus Christ—the title itself is not the litmus test.[19]

Robinson argues that since Protestants and Catholics are willing to tolerate and accept one another even though differences exist, why not grant the same respect to Mormons? What Robinson fails to comprehend is that no true Christian willingly assigns the title "Christian" to anyone simply on the basis of belonging to a particular church or denomination: whether it is evangelical, protestant, or Catholic. One can be a Baptist or a Presbyterian or a Lutheran or a Methodist or a Catholic and not be a Christian. True Christians are those who have met personal faith requirements set forth by the New Testament. It is not membership in a particular church that is significant, but what a person believes about Christ that is of the utmost importance.

---

17. This is Robinson's preferred terminology of LDS people.

18. Robinson, *Are Mormons Christians?*, vii. Italics included in the original.

19. For example, The "Christian Science" movement is neither "Christian" nor "scientific."

A more important question might be, "What do you believe about Jesus?" Robinson seeks to address this issue, suggesting that Mormons do believe in the Christ of the New Testament. Robinson writes, "The Latter-day Saints have a very high Christology."[20]

> Latter-day Saints believe that Jesus is the pre-existent Word of the Father who became the literal, physical, genetic Son of God. As the pre-existent Word he was the agent of the Father in the creation of all things. As the glorified Son he is the agent of the Father in the salvation of all humanity.[21]

At first glance these statements seem reasonable and very "Christian." Notice the phrase "genetic Son of God." Did you catch that? Robinson teaches that Jesus is the literal, offspring of God. Jesus was physically conceived by the god, Elohim,[22] in exactly the same way as you and I were by our parents. However, this is not the only difference. Study Robinson's definitions carefully and you will see that, even by his own definitions, Mormonism brings a much different Jesus to us. Christ was preexistent, but so were the rest of us.[23] Jesus helped in the creation of this world, but he is not the Creator God of the universe. Jesus is not "God," but one of many gods.[24] Robinson even suggests that Jesus progressed to godhood in a manner which we should imitate.[25]

While the LDS Church does bear the name Jesus Christ, Mormonism does not bring us "another testament of Jesus,"[26] but presents to us a much different Jesus—a counterfeit Christ. Paul addresses this in 2 Corinthians:

> But I am afraid that just as Eve was deceived by the serpent's cunning, your minds may somehow be led astray from your

---

20. Robinson, *Are Mormons Christians?*, 113.

21. Ibid.

22. In Mormonism, God the Father is named Elohim while God the Son is named Jehovah.

23. Robinson, *Are Mormons Christians?*, 104.

24. Ibid., 65.

25. Ibid., 60.

26. This is the claim from the cover of The Book of Mormon.

sincere and pure devotion to Christ. For if someone comes to you and preaches a Jesus other than the Jesus we preached, or if you receive a different spirit from the one you received, or a different gospel from the one you accepted, you put up with it easily enough.[27]

Note clearly, it is not anti-Mormon argumentation (as Robinson suggests) that excludes the LDS from the Christian faith, but their own beliefs about Jesus. Robinson himself espouses in this book many of the very issues that do actually separate Christianity and Mormonism: the plurality of gods, the literal fatherhood and sonship of Christ, the fallibility and incompleteness of Scripture, the open canon, the deification of man, the authority of the Mormon priesthood, pre-mortal existence, exaltation by works, etc. Each of these stated doctrines lands Mormonism well outside the ranks of mainstream Christianity regardless of Robinson's profession otherwise.[28]

We clearly discover in reading this book, that while Mormonism often uses the same vocabulary as mainstream Christianity, the meaning of these words is much different. We must conclude from this particular work (apart from the desire to be known as Christian) little has changed within the LDS church.

---

27. 2 Corinthians 11:3-4, NIV.

28. Imagine how a Mormon might respond to the following statement. "I'm a Mormon, but I don't believe Joseph Smith was a true prophet of God. I'm a Mormon, but I don't believe that God was once a man or that men can become gods. I'm a Mormon, but I don't believe the Mormon Church is the only true church or that the Book of Mormon is the Word of God." A knowledgeable Latter-day Saint would defy that such a person was indeed Mormon. Why? Because the person who claims to be Mormon denies the very doctrines that make Mormons what they are. At the same time, a Mormon who claims to be Christian, and yet denies the very doctrines that makes a Christian, places them outside of Christianity.

3

Growing Uncertainty

> *"I would personally just like to find some Evangelicals willing to admit the truth—that Mormons accept the New Testament and worship the Christ who is described there."*[1]
>
> —Stephen E. Robinson

ROBINSON'S BOOK *Are Mormon's Christian?*[2] created an array of discussion among Mormons and evangelicals alike. In response to the public outcry from Robinson's book, Greg Johnson of *Standing Together* convinced Stephen Robinson and Craig Blomberg[3] to jointly write about the differences between Mormonism and Christianity. In 1997, they coauthored, *How Wide the Divide? A Mormon and an Evangelical in Conversation.* To my knowledge, this is the first time an evangelical scholar and a Mormon author have jointly written about their respective faiths.

As previously stated, these efforts at dialogue should be applauded, yet it should also be recognized that it has and will continue to create a controversy in some circles by those who believe the lines between Christianity and Mormonism are somehow blurred.[4] Those who see doctrinal differences marginalized by

---

1. Blomberg and Robinson, *How Wide the Divide?*, 20.

2. Reviewed in previous chapter.

3. Craig Blomberg is the professor of New Testament at Denver Seminary and the author of numerous books on the Gospels, inspiration of Scripture, etc.

4. Some evangelicals have been disappointed with Blomberg, feeling that

this work need to revisit it and reexamine the definition of terms. Read this book carefully and you will discover that the divide is indeed wide and the gap between Mormonism and mainstream Christianity does not appear to be shrinking.

The authors focus on four foundational issues of disagreement: Scripture; the nature of God and the deification of believers; the deity of Christ and the Trinity; and salvation and the eternal state.[5] Once again, Robinson seeks to present the case that Mormonism has been misrepresented and is deserving of the title, Christian.

While the style of writing in this book is obviously much different from his previous work—sharing the page with evangelical scholar Craig Blomberg, Robinson's arguments are primarily the same as that of his book, *Are Mormons Christians?* Not unlike the first, Robinson[6] hopes to persuade his readers that Mormonism has been unfairly demonized and if understood properly would be viewed as Christian.

Robinson starts with the wrong foot forward, however, when he writes, "It is a rare thing indeed for non-Mormons writing about the Saints to get it right even when they are trying to, and most contemporary non-LDS writing on the Mormons is frankly *not* trying to get it right."[7] Immediately, we perceive some of Robinson's agenda. Does he truly think that all non-Mormon writers are to be viewed as intentionally maligning the Mormon faith? Are all who disagree with his position guilty of slander and deceit?[8] Robinson

---

he conceded some important points. My position is that Blomberg did a remarkable job dealing with key principles while maintaining a charitable attitude in matters of lesser importance.

5. Blomberg and Robinson, *How Wide the Divide?*, 25.

6. I will be consistently referring to Robinson in this work rather than to Blomberg and Robinson. This is not an attempt to overlook Blomberg or minimize his contribution. It merely stems from the fact that for the most part I agree with Blomberg and am at odds with Robinson.

7. Blomberg and Robinson, *How Wide the Divide?*, 14.

8. This seems to fall into his category of exclusion by name calling.

continues, "The worst way for evangelicals to learn about Latter-day Saints is to ask other non-Mormons or to read non-Mormon literature about the Saints."[9] This type of unsubstantiated attack seems out of place, especially in a work hoping to produce conversation and dialogue.

Two other issues need mentioning before we can delve into the contents of *How Wide the Divide?* We must clarify two subtle techniques used by Robinson. First, Robinson once again tries to limit the playing field of analysis to the standard works of the church.[10] On the surface, this request seems not only entirely reasonable, but absolutely essential. Why should Mormonism be critiqued and judged by material outside of the authoritative teachings of Mormonism? Hasn't much been written by Christian authors that Christian churches would disagree with?

What Robinson is suggesting, however, is not only inconsistent with what Mormonism teaches,[11] but goes against the authoritative works he claims are binding. In one fell swoop, Robinson not only deems unofficial much of what is clearly recognized and taught as doctrine in LDS circles, but also makes "unofficial" what canonical Mormonism (the standard works) defines as the highest authority in the Mormon church—the living prophets. Robinson himself knows this to be true when he writes:

> The direct revelation to a prophet or apostle is immediate and primary, and this is the word of God in the purest sense—as word and hearing rather than as text . . . For Latter-day Saints, the church's guarantee of doctrinal correctness lies primarily in the living prophet, and only secondarily in the preserva-

9. Blomberg and Robinson, *How Wide the Divide?*, 15.

10. While I have dealt with this in the review of *Are Mormons Christians?* Robinson includes more material here that deserves attention.

11. Mormons are told repeatedly that God will not allow church leaders to lead them astray. In church manuals they are told to trust the First Presidency and the Quorum of the Twelve.

tion of the written text. This is, after all, the New Testament model.[12]

If direct revelation to a prophet is God's word in the purest sense, should we not look to the current prophet of the church as well as past prophets to see what they have written?[13] Yet, Robinson insists that we not consult LDS works like Bruce McConkie's *Mormon Doctrine* or the *Journal of Discourses* which is an approved LDS collection of nineteenth-century sermons from the past prophets of the church.[14] Once again, Robinson wants to limit the material that can be used by non-Mormons to the standard works of the church or at least current[15] approved LDS material. Robinson, however, makes dozens of references to former Prophets, Apostles, Mormon authors, and unauthorized sources throughout this work to make his points.

The second subtle technique is Robinson's use of Christian terms. We have already pointed out that Christianity and Mormonism often use the same words, but define these words very differently. Robinson recognizes this as well.

> Another obstacle to mutual understanding is *terminology*—our respective theological vocabularies. Latter-day Saints and Evangelicals generally employ the same theological terms, but we usually define them differently, and this quite often makes communication more difficult than if we spoke different religious languages entirely. The similarity of terms makes us *think*

---

12. Blomberg and Robinson, *How Wide the Divide?*, 57.

13. Interestingly enough, even the published writings of the current Prophet of the LDS Church contain the disclaimer disavowing its content as officially representing the LDS church. Here is the standard disclaimer. "This work is not an official publication of The Church of Jesus Christ of Latter-day Saints. The views expressed herein are the responsibility of the author and do not necessarily represent the position of the Church."

14. Blomberg and Robinson, *How Wide the Divide?*, 73.

15. Why is it necessary to use words like "current" if LDS leaders are in fact getting their information from an unchanging God?

> we are communicating, but when all is said and done both
> sides go away with the feeling that nothing quite added up.[16]

What Robinson is saying is true, and yet, throughout this work, Robinson intentionally uses terminology that he knows will be misconstrued by evangelicals. He suggests that Mormons believe in God, Jesus, salvation, etc., using the same words but failing to make clarifications and the distinctions that are needed. Take for example his summary of beliefs. Paraphrasing Joseph Smith he says, "We believe in God, the Eternal Father, and in God's Son, Jesus Christ, and in the Holy Ghost. We accept the biblical doctrine that God is three and that God is one."[17] On the surface, this sounds very good. Could it be that Mormonism is shifting? As you read elsewhere in this work, however, you realize that Robinson, like Millet, defines "eternal" as a long period of time. He defines "son" as a literal offspring of God the Father, and "one" to mean one in purpose. You must read carefully and critically to decipher what Robinson really means when he uses Christian terms.

> Latter-day Saints also believe in the *literal* fatherhood of God
> and the brotherhood of humanity. We believe that God and
> humans are the same species of being and that all men and
> women were his spiritual offspring in a premortal existence.[18]

Examples could be repeated many times and include almost every point which Christians hold sacred.

When it comes to imprecise definitions, Robinson does acknowledge a lack of training on the part of the nonprofessional clergy of the LDS Church, but also places blame on the shoulders of evangelicals for inadequate communication and highly idiomatic terminology.[19] Robinson fails to acknowledge or admit that

---

16. Blomberg and Robinson, *How Wide the Divide?*, 13. Italics included in the original.

17. Ibid., 16.

18. Ibid., 18. Italics included in the original.

19. Ibid., 15.

the major causes of misunderstandings are essentially due to the intentional redefinition of biblical words and concepts by advocates of Mormonism.[20]

With these subtle techniques in mind, we will now turn our attention to the main issues addressed by this book.

Scripture

When it comes to Scripture, two major issues divide Mormonism and Christianity. Blomberg correctly summarizes the first when he says, "One of the main issues separating Evangelicals and Mormons is whether or not the Old and New Testaments constitute the sum total of God's scriptural revelation to humanity."[21] In addition to the Bible, Mormons recognize the Book of Mormon, the Doctrine and Covenants, and the Pearl of Great Price as Scripture. At stake is the issue of whether or not the canon of Scripture is open or closed. Mormons not only hold to a much larger canon, but submit that God continues to speak today to his prophets.[22]

The second major issue centers around inerrancy. "Inerrancy means that when all facts are known, the Scriptures in their original autographs and properly interpreted will be shown to be wholly true in everything that they affirm, whether that has to do with

---

20. This process of redefinition reminds me of what is happening currently in our country with the word "marriage." Marriage has always been a covenant between a man and a woman. Those who do not like this definition are seeking to redefine it. Words mean something and we should not simply redefine words to our liking, especially when it blurs and contaminates communication.

21. Blomberg and Robinson, *How Wide the Divide?*, 38.

22. Mormon Apostle James Talmage writes: "We believe that God is as willing today as He ever has been to reveal His mind and will to man, and that He does so through His appointed servants—prophets, seers, and revelators—invested through ordination with the authority of the Holy Priesthood. We rely therefore on the teachings of the living oracles of God as of equal validity with the doctrines of the written word" (James E. Talmage, *The Articles of Faith*, 7).

doctrine or morality or with the social, physical or life sciences."[23] Robinson responds that "the church's guarantee of doctrinal correctness lies primarily in the living prophet, and only secondarily in the preservation of the written text"[24] and "what God has said to the apostles and prophets in the past is always secondary to what God is saying directly to his apostles and prophets now."[25] This leads Robinson to conclude, "If the original wording is misleading, rewrite it; if the original reading is ambiguous, clarify it."[26] Mormons hold that neither the Bible, nor Mormon scriptures are without error or God's complete revelation to us today.[27]

When discussing the issue of Mormon scriptures, Robinson uses two additional arguments in an attempt to convince the reader that additional Scripture should not banish Mormonism from the ranks of Christianity. First, he suggests that since there is no consensus among Christians as to what constitutes Scripture, Mormonism cannot be excluded from among them. Second, he argues that an open canon, with God adding to Scripture, is not necessarily contradictory to the Bible. Therefore, he concludes, Mormonism cannot be rejected on the grounds of an open canon. What Robinson fails to consider is that even if additional Scripture does not in theory invalidate Mormonism (and I'm not willing to grant this premise), the fact that additional Mormon scripture contradicts what the Bible clearly teaches does nullify its claims.[28]

---

23. Blomberg and Robinson, *How Wide the Divide?*, 34.

24. Ibid., 56.

25. Ibid., 59.

26. Ibid., 65.

27. When speaking specifically about the Bible, the Book of Mormon, and the Doctrine and Covenants, President Wilford Woodruff said, "When compared with the living oracles those books are nothing to me; those books do not convey the word of God direct to us now, as do the words of a Prophet or a man bearing the Holy Priesthood in our days and generation. I would rather have the living oracles than all the writing in the books" (Ezra Taft Benson, *The Teachings of Ezra Taft Benson*, 4).

28. Not to mention that the LDS canon contradicts itself.

God and Deification

The second topic of discussion addressed by Blomberg and Robinson centers around the issue of what God is like. There is no more important area of discussion than this,[29] but once again, terminology plays an important and defining role. As Robinson depicts the Mormon God, he gives this description: "In the LDS view God is omniscient, omnipotent, omnipresent, infinite, eternal and unchangeable."[30] He quotes the Doctrine and Covenants which says, "Father, Son, and Holy Ghost are one God, infinite and eternal, without end."[31] While this seems very orthodox, do not think for a moment that these words represent mainstream Christianity. Look a little farther and you will learn that the God of Mormonism had a physical body and was once a man.

> Nothing I say here should be interpreted as denying the importance for Mormonism of God's corporeality and God's nature as an exalted man. Neither am I denying the importance of LDS belief that we humans are literally God's children and can become what God is. These are linchpins in LDS theology.[32]

In other words, Robinson is saying, when I define God as omniscient, omnipotent, omnipresent, infinite, eternal and unchangeable, don't interpret those as meaning omniscient, omnipotent, omnipresent, infinite, eternal and unchangeable. The linchpins of LDS theology describe God as an exalted man who has a body of flesh and blood and people are literally God's children who can become God. Infinite must mean finite, eternal is simply a long time, and unchangeable must be redefined to mean God hasn't changed in purpose. Even words like omnipresent must take on new meaning because God has a body of flesh and blood. Robinson says, "While God in the LDS view is not *physically* present in all things

---

29. I would put the issue of Christ on this same level.

30. Blomberg and Robinson, *How Wide the Divide?*, 77.

31. Doctrine and Covenants, 20:28.

32. Blomberg and Robinson, *How Wide the Divide?*, 91.

but rather spiritually present, I don't think this really differs much from the evangelical view."[33] How do you justify such a statement? Robinson's answer: "Latter-day Saints affirm only that the Father has a body, not that his body has him."[34] This is nothing more than linguistic nonsense.

Realizing that suggesting God was once a man might alienate Christians, Robinson writes: "To those who are offended by Joseph Smith's suggestion that God the Father was once, before the beginning, a man, I point out that God the Son was undoubtedly once a man, and that did not compromise his divinity."[35]

Robinson fails to distinguish between God (an infinite being) placing restrictions upon himself and man (a finite being) becoming something much greater than himself. He also fails to see the ramifications of a finite God. At this point Blomberg responds impressively.

> There seems to be no way for finite beings *by themselves* ever to become infinite. It is one thing for an infinite God to voluntarily restrict himself to certain limitations of finitude. It is quite another for a finite being to become infinite unless by means of some more powerful agent.[36]

Robinson's answer to Blomberg is that a god before this god helped him become infinite. Blomberg shows the fallacy of this argument as well. "We find ourselves in the logical quagmire of asking who created those gods, and so on, ad infinitum."[37]

One more observation should be made about Robinson's arguments before going on. Robinson suggests that the Mormon doctrine of man becoming god is not unbiblical. He gives biblical references and cites early church fathers and makes them sound like they give credence to the view that God the Father was once a

---

33. Ibid., 77. Italics included in the original.

34. Ibid., 88.

35. Ibid., 91.

36. Ibid., 105. Italics included in the original.

37. Ibid., 105.

mere mortal. Robinson fails to note that every passage and reference he mentions refers not to a prehistoric period in which God was once a man before becoming God, but to the period of the incarnation before Christ regained his rightful place in heaven.[38]

Christ and the Trinity

Robinson suggests that the Christ of Mormonism is the Christ of the Bible, just not the Christ of the Hellenistic church as defined by fourth and fifth century church councils.

> That God is somehow simultaneously three and one I have no doubt because the Bible and the Book of Mormon both tell me so, but I do not trust the intellectuals of the Hellenistic church to have figured out exactly *how* this is so, nor do I invest their theories with the authority of Scripture.[39]

Robinson avows that Mormons believe in God, Jesus Christ, and in the Holy Ghost. "However, we believe that the oneness of these three is not an ontological oneness of being (this is a *creedal* rather than a *biblical* affirmation), but a oneness of mind, purpose, power and intent."[40] He rejects the idea that God, Jesus, and the Holy Spirit are ontologically one being. Robinson states rather emphatically that the three remain separate beings with separate and individual bodies.[41]

In response to Robinson's accusation that the ontological unity of the Godhood was a later pollution of the early church creeds, Blomberg says:

> It is important to observe that within the first five centuries of intense Christian discussion about the nature of God, tritheism was never nearly the temptation that unitarianism was. In other words, as Christians wrestled with how to keep the three persons of the Trinity both separate and unified, they far more

38. Ibid., 89.

39. Ibid., 128. Italics included in the original.

40. Ibid., 129. Italics included in the original.

41. Ibid., 130.

commonly erred on the side of *not* adequately distinguishing the three. No early Christian theologian ever identified Jesus as a completely separate God from Yahweh . . . that would have surely violated monotheism.[42]

Robinson asserts that the early creeds corrupted the church and that if we returned to the first century teaching of the church before the arrival of the creeds, we would find teaching that resembles the Mormon doctrine of Christ. This is just not true, nor is it a change from traditional Mormonism. Joseph Smith's first vision recounts:

> My object in going to inquire of the Lord was to know which of all the sects was right, that I might know which to join . . . I was answered that I must join none of them, for they were all wrong; and the Personage who addressed me said that all their creeds were an abomination in his sight; that those professors were all corrupt; that: "they draw near to me with their lips, but their hearts are far from me."[43]

While Robinson would like us to believe that it was the early creeds of the church that perverted Christian theology, it must be pointed out that one cannot find LDS theology in the teachings of any theologian of the early church, either before or after Nicea. No one ever taught that Jesus was the firstborn spirit of God the father. No church father ever suggested that Jesus was the literal offspring of God. No first century author ever suggested that God was once a mortal man or that he has a physical body. The early church creeds did not introduce heresy, but it was the intent of those early church creeds to insulate the church from heresy. Had Mormon theology appeared on the scene around the time of the Nicene creed, the creed would have undoubtedly addressed this false teaching.

A further departure is found when Robinson describes the difference between God and Jesus. As noted earlier, Mormons believe that God the Father is named Elohim while Christ is named Jehovah.

---

42. Ibid., 116.

43. Pearl of Great Price, 1:5–19.

> For us Christ is not a being separate from the Jehovah of
> the Old Testament—we identify Christ as Jehovah, the God
> of Abraham, Isaac and Jacob . . . We believe that almost all
> references to "God" or to "the Father" in the Old Testament,
> and many in the New, refer specifically to God the Son, Jesus
> Christ.[44]

This becomes a significant problem when studying biblical texts
that describe God using both references simultaneously.

When it comes to the virgin birth, Robinson asserts his belief
in this doctrine, but then writes. "Mary was in some unspecified
manner made pregnant by God the Father." This was "not in viola-
tion of natural law."[45]

> If Jesus was truly a *human* being, then he had forty-six chro-
> mosomes, a double strand of twenty-three. If he was truly
> human, he got one strand of twenty-three chromosomes from
> his mother. Where did the other strand come from, if not
> from his Father?[46]

Robinson admits that much of what Mormonism teaches
about Christ is not found in Scripture, but also suggests it is
not unscriptural. He admits that Mormonism has a different
doctrine of the trinity and a different view of the origin and nature of Christ, even a different concept about the virgin birth,
but maintains that they do not worship a different Christ. Yet,
Mormonism's own Prophet, Gordon B. Hinckley[47] says, "The traditional Christ of whom they [non-Mormons] speak is not the
Christ of whom I speak."[48]

---

44. Blomberg and Robinson, *How Wide the Divide?*, 134.

45. Ibid., 135.

46. Ibid., 139. Italics included in the original.

47. Hinckley is the current Prophet of the church and has been serving
since 1995.

48. LDS *Church News Week*, June 20, 1998, p. 7.

Salvation

When it comes to the issue of salvation, Robinson readily accepts that there are significant differences. "I would object to any claim that the differences between us are trivial or inconsequential."[49] I would wholeheartedly agree and even suggest that the differences are not only immense but in many ways complete opposites.

Heaven and Hell are different. Hell is only "a temporary state to which spirits are consigned between death and resurrection."[50] During this period, people will be tested and given the opportunity to respond to Christ and even obtain a degree of glory.[51]

Heaven is different as well:

> Mormons believe the saved will be divided into three broad divisions called kingdoms or glories. The lowest of these is the telestial glory, which is reserved for those who were wicked in the flesh (both LDS and non-LDS) but who . . . in some sense and to some degree turned to Christ . . . The next highest glory, the terrestrial kingdom, is reserved for the honorable men and women of the earth, the "righteous," who rejected the fullness of the gospel and the witness of the Holy Spirit during their mortal lives but changed their minds in spirit prison . . . The highest degree of heavenly glory is the celestial kingdom.[52]

When it comes to the actual act of salvation, Mormonism, on the surface, shows signs of similarity. But general salvation is the doctrine that Christ's death on the cross secured only a measure of salvation. Through Jesus, all people will be raised to experience a better existence. Jesus only purchased the ability to be resurrected.[53]

---

49. Blomberg and Robinson, *How Wide the Divide?*, 163.

50. Ibid., 150.

51. Ibid., 152.

52. Ibid.

53. This, too, is not a change from traditional Mormonism. Mormon theologian and apostle Bruce McConkie has written, "Unconditional or general salvation, that which comes by grace alone without obedience to gospel law, consists in the mere fact of being resurrected." McConkie, *Mormon Doctrine*, 669.

Once again, we quickly see that little besides terminology has changed within Mormonism. Robinson defines: Scripture as fallible and incomplete; God as a mortal man who progressed to becoming God; Jesus as the literal son of God and procreated being; salvation as exaltation to godhood; gospel as keeping the law and ordinances of the Mormon church; and, grace as God's help after all that you can do.

After reading Robinson, I must conclude that little besides terminology has changed. What Robinson espouses is nothing more than the traditional teaching of the LDS Church couched in evangelical terminology. But while it appears that Robinson remains firmly established within the ranks of traditional Mormonism, I still had hopes that my new friend, Dr. Millet, might represent significant change within the Mormon system.

4

Finally, Some Clear Answers

"What makes us different from most other Christians in the way we read and use the Bible and other scriptures is our belief in continuing revelation."[1]

—Robert Millet

WHILE VISITING with Dr. Millet after the third dialogue at Eagle Christian Church, he graciously gave me an autographed copy of his most recent book, *A Different Jesus?* This, more than any other source, has provided the answer to the question I've been asking: Is Mormonism changing? It is interesting that the man, who in part, prompted my quest for this answer, has also brought me to my conclusion.

As I began to read this book, I hoped to find new and refreshing information about the Mormon view of things. I did not expect complete restoration (nothing changes overnight), but I longed for a hint of fresh thinking and new direction, if not within the leadership of the LDS Church, at least from a prominent member from within their sphere of influence. Knowing that Dr. Millet expressed disappointment that many refuse to accept Mormons as Christians, I expected arguments for inclusion of the LDS within the ranks of Christianity.

While I hoped to see change, I had prepared myself for the worst. Thinking that Dr. Millet was writing to gain approval from

---

1. Millet, *A Different Jesus?*, 16.

the evangelical community,[2] I acknowledged the possibility that I would find garbled descriptions and cloudy definitions that would only further muddy the distinction instead of bringing clarity to this issue. As I read the opening pages, I anticipated more of the same material I had encountered in the books previously discussed. But what I found was unexpected. Dr. Millet readily admitted that the LDS are "Christian but different."[3]

More than an admission of significant differences, Dr. Millet willingly embraced traditional LDS doctrine. Unlike the previous dialogues and conversations in which he minimized differences and accentuated similarities, Dr. Millet stated "without hesitation that there are differences between us. Were this not so, there would have been no need for a restoration of the gospel."[4] For the first time in my experience with him, Dr. Millet's belief that the LDS Church contains the only true faith rang out loud and clear.

> The Saints feel that the Church of Jesus Christ fell away after the death of the apostles and the keys of authority were lost to the world for almost two millennia. Thus the call of Joseph Smith signaled not only a restoration of divine truths, but also a restoration of the powers necessary to reestablish the Kingdom of God on earth, this time to remain forever.[5]

Dr. Millet said emphatically, "that apostasy entailed the loss or corruption of *divine authority* and *true doctrine*."[6] With a belief in the loss of authority and truth, Dr. Millet proceeds by mentioning topic after topic in which Mormonism has attempted to correct the mistaken views of evangelical Christianity. These supposed corrections not only place Mormonism outside of evangelical Christianity, but demonstrate that Mormonism has not changed significantly in regards to doctrine in recent years. Let me highlight those areas

---

2. Notice this book is published by Eerdmans Publishing Co.

3. Millet, *A Different Jesus?*, 170.

4. Ibid., 171.

5. Ibid., 76.

6. Ibid., 39. Italics included in the original.

which place Mormonism at odds with Christianity, while at the same time demonstrate that Mormonism has not strayed from its historic roots.[7] I have responded to most of these issues previously in this work, but it is important to clarify Dr. Millet's position and establish him within mainstream Mormonism.

Premortal Existence

This is where everything begins in Mormonism. Dr. Millet accepts the Mormon view that everything existed in a state of preexistence before it was formed here on earth. "From a Latter-day Saint perspective, humankind did not suddenly spring into existence at the time of their mortal birth. We have always lived."[8] Dr. Millet continues:

> To be sure, Joseph Smith taught that man is an eternal being. He declared that the intelligence of man "is not a created being; it existed from eternity, and will exist to eternity. Anything created cannot be eternal."[9]

Dr. Millet not only demonstrates his beliefs that mankind lived in a previous life in a spirit world, but also makes reference to the Mormon doctrine of formation, rather than creation.[10] He speaks of men and women as the literal offspring of God.

> Latter-day Saints believe that men and women are the spirit sons and daughters of God, that we lived in a premortal existence before birth, that we grew and expanded in the "first estate" . . . in that world men and women were separate and distinct spirit personages, had consciousness, volition, maleness and femaleness, and moral agency. Thus God is literally our spirit Father, and we inherit from him divine qualities and attributes. In the long expanse of time before we were born

---

7. I will document historic teachings of Mormonism in the next chapter of this work.

8. Millet, *A Different Jesus?*, 18.

9. Ibid., 83.

10. God did not create man, because man's spirit has eternally existed.

into mortality, the spirit sons and daughters of God developed talents, strengths, and capacities.[11]

Not only are these radical departures from evangelical Christianity, but well established doctrines firmly grounded in historic LDS teaching.

God, Jesus and Humanity

Dr. Millet sets forth his belief that God was once a man who progressed to godhood and is still contained within a body of flesh and blood.[12] While admitting that God had a body in his dialogues, he provides a unique twist to the creation account of Genesis. Dr. Millet suggests that God was once a man because man was made in the image of God's body. Quoting from the Book of Moses within the Pearl of Great Price, he says, "In the likeness of God made he him; in the image of his own body, male and female, created he them."[13]

> Latter-day scripture states unequivocally that God is a man, a Man of Holiness (Moses 6:57) who possesses a body of flesh and bones (D&C 130:22). These concepts are clearly a part of what Mormons call the doctrinal restoration.[14]

According to Dr. Millet, God was once a man like us, and we were formed in the image of his body. But before we lived on earth, we lived in the spirit realm. Millet affirms that Jesus, too, began as a spirit child, became a man, and then evolved into God. "As a premortal spirit, Jehovah grew in knowledge and power to the point where he became 'like unto God.'"[15] He clearly espouses Mormon doctrine when he writes:

---

11. Millet, *A Different Jesus?*, 19.

12. "That which is without body, parts, and passions is nothing. There is no God in heaven but that God who has flesh and bones." Ibid., 145.

13. Book of Moses 6:8–9.

14. Millet, *A Different Jesus?*, 144.

15. Millet, *A Different Jesus?*, 73.

> Jesus was the firstborn spirit child of God the Father and thus
> the recipient of the birthright of the royal family. As such,
> and in that premortal realm, he was the Elder Brother of all
> the spirit sons and daughters of the Father . . . Over the ages
> in that premortal world Christ grew in light and truth and
> knowledge and power.[16]

Born as a spirit child of God, Jesus would later become the physical son of God. Dr. Millet writes, "Jesus of Nazareth is literally the Son of God . . . He is not the Son of the Father in some mystical, metaphorical sense."[17]

Not only is Jesus both the spiritual and the physical child of God, we are no different. "Thus God is literally our spirit Father, and we inherit from him divine qualities and attributes."[18] Millet affirms what Mormonism has always taught: every man, woman, and child is a spirit brother of Jesus and because of their divine qualities, should be considered on a path to godhood. Dr. Millet regards this teaching as an honorable doctrine which should be regarded as necessary for the restoration of Christian faith.

> The Church of Jesus Christ of Latter-day Saints gladly teaches
> and declares the Christian doctrine that all men and women
> are brothers and sisters, not only by blood relationship from
> common mortal progenitors, but also as literal spirit children
> of an Eternal Father.[19]

In addition to these heretical teachings about both the Father and the Son, Dr. Millet affirms yet another distinctive of the LDS church. "He [Jesus] was the Great Jehovah of the Old Testament, the Messiah of the New."[20] Dr. Millet believes and teaches that most of the references to God in the Old Testament actually speak about Jesus in his pre-incarnate state.[21]

---

16. Ibid., 20.
17. Ibid., 74.
18. Ibid., 19.
19. Ibid., 65.
20. Ibid., 187.
21. This position seems to be inconsistent with the Mormon doctrine of

Grace and Salvation

When it comes to salvation, Dr. Millet has continually affirmed that salvation is only available by the grace of God. When recounting a conversation in New England,[22] Dr. Millet was asked, "You are standing before the judgment bar of the Almighty, and God turns to you and asks: 'Robert Millet, what right do you have to enter heaven? Why should I let you in?'" Dr. Millet responded, "because of my complete trust in and reliance upon the merits and mercy and grace of the Lord Jesus Christ."[23] This seems like the appropriate answer, and yet, a close examination reveals that both grace and salvation are much different in Millet's thinking than in an evangelical understanding.

Millet describes the salvation which Jesus purchases as only a universal salvation which enables men to face judgement. Because of Jesus' resurrection, all men will rise, but each will still face judgement. Notice what Millet says. "Latter-day Saints believe in a type of universal salvation, [but] not in the sense that everyone will one day dwell with God and be like God."[24] There is a distinction between the universal salvation (immortality) purchased by Christ, and an individual's salvation which requires work on the behalf of each person. When Millet says, "saved by grace," he is speaking only of a universal salvation that brings forth a person from the grave. While he believes that grace will be extended to each person to give them the opportunity to face judgement, the individual's salvation is ultimately based on what they do, either in this life, or in the time period before the resurrection when they can still be redeemed by what they learn and how they respond.

Eternal Progression in which Jesus progressed to Godhood after becoming a man.

22. I believe this conversation was held with Dr. Haddon Robinson and he is the one who asked this insightful question.

23. Millet, *A Different Jesus?*, 177.

24. Millet, *A Different Jesus?*, 108.

Millet writes, "Learning and growth and redemption continue well beyond the grave."[25]

> From an LDS perspective, there are two types of salvation . . . universal and individual. Universal salvation is from physical death, a salvation available to all. *Immortality* is salvation from the grave . . . it is a universal gift. Individual salvation is another matter. Though all salvation is available through the goodness and grace of Christ, there are certain things that must be done in order for divine grace and mercy to be activated.[26]

While resurrection from the grave (universal salvation) is purchased for all by Christ and applied by grace, individual salvation:

> Requires all the atonement of Christ, the mercy of the Father, the pity of angels and the grace of the Lord Jesus Christ to be with us always, and then to do the very best we possibly can, to get rid of the sin within us, so that we may escape from this world into the celestial kingdom.[27]

Notice Dr. Millet's definition of grace. We must rely on the grace of Jesus AND do all we can to get rid of the sin within us. He says elsewhere, "We must work to our limit and then rely upon the merits, mercy, and grace of the Holy One."[28] Grace only makes up for our deficiencies and can only be applied after we do all we can do.

This is in keeping with traditional Mormon doctrine that suggests that Jesus purchased the ability to be resurrected, but assigns individuals with the responsibility to work for their own salvation. This working can take place either in this life, or in the life to come. Millet writes, "For those who have not received this gospel, the opportunity will come to them in a life hereafter."[29]

---

25. Ibid., 109.

26. Ibid., 95. Italics included in the original.

27. Ibid., 88. Notice, this is a quotation from the *Journal of Discourses* 11:301. Both Robinson and Millet have repeatedly urged their readers not to quote from this source as official doctrine.

28. Ibid., 69.

29. Ibid., 65.

"In short, Latter-day Saints believe that all men and women will be granted the opportunity to receive the gospel of Jesus Christ, either in this life or in the life that continues after one's mortal death."[30] Ultimate salvation (exaltation), for a Mormon, is not simply experiencing resurrection (which is available to all through Christ), nor is it attaining some level of heaven (which is available to most), but consists of the continuation of the family unit and inheriting and possessing the fulness of the glory of God.[31] Millet quotes President Gordon B. Hinckley as saying, "The whole design of the gospel is to lead us onward and upward to greater achievement, even, eventually to Godhood."[32]

Scripture and Authority

Another area of departure that needs to be addressed in this section relates to Dr. Millet's view of the Bible, other scripture, the prophets, and what the church considers to be the ultimate source of authority. Once again, Dr. Millet is firmly camped within the historic teachings of the LDS Church.

Dr. Millet boldly says, "Latter-day Saints do not subscribe to a position of scriptural inerrancy."[33] While Mormons believe that the Bible contains God's word, they also believe that the material previously given contained all the information they were prepared to receive at that time.[34] Latter-day Saints do not believe the Scriptures are limited to the sixty-six books of the Bible, nor do they believe that the Bible now contains all that it once did.[35] Nor do Mormons believe that the Book of Mormon, the Doctrine and Covenants, or the Pearl of Great Price complete his revelation.

---

30. Ibid., 76.

31. Ibid., 115.

32. Ibid., 117.

33. Ibid., 37. See also page 45.

34. Ibid., 45.

35. Ibid., 46.

> Latter-day Saints hold a view of canon that does not restrict
> itself to God's revelations of the past, whether they be those
> which they revere in common with their fellow Christians or
> those believed uniquely by the Saints. Their view is broader:
> the canon is not closed, nor will it ever be. To them, revelation
> has not ceased; it continues in the Church. Further revelation
> is not only viewed as theoretically possible; it is needed and
> expected.[36]

Dr. Millet readily affirms that when the Mormons read and
use their Bibles (and other Scriptures) they do so differently from
evangelicals. "For us, the Scriptures are not the ultimate source
of knowledge, but what precedes the ultimate source."[37] The most
important knowledge is not written revelation, but current revelation. The benefit derived from the reading and studying of ancient
Scriptures is simply to prepare one to realize how God has spoken,
to better comprehend him when he gives personal revelation.

> Latter-day Saints believe the scriptures are to be read and
> searched and studied; the reader of scripture is encouraged
> to open himself or herself to inspiration and to 'liken the
> scriptures' unto their own life situation. In short, though the
> study of scripture may not be considered a sacramental act,
> Latter-day Saints believe that one essential key to the receipt
> of *individual* revelation—to know the mind and will of God
> in one's life, and to come to know God—is the study of *insti-
> tutional* revelation.[38]

Not only do the Mormons not believe in the scriptural inerrancy of the Bible,[39] they don't consider their own scriptures or
prophets to be infallible, either.

> While Latter-day Saints admire and respect and even revere
> their church leaders, we do not believe in prophetic or apostolic

36. Ibid., 10.

37. Ibid., 16.

38. Ibid., 16. Italics included in the original.

39. Mormon Apostle Orson Pratt said, ". . . who, in his right mind, could,
for one moment, suppose the Bible in its present form to be a perfect guide?
Who knows that even one verse of the Bible has escaped pollution?" (*Divine
Authenticity of the Book of Mormon*, 47).

infallibility . . . they are God's covenant spokesmen, authorized and empowered to declare his word and lead his children, but they are not perfect.[40]

This is a rather interesting admission when you consider that Dr. Millet also affirms, "Doctrinal finality rests with apostles and prophets."[41] Dr. Millet suggests that "there is a great advantage to a priesthood hierarchy as a means of maintaining doctrinal orthodoxy,"[42] in fact he demands that the restoration of the church required the restoration of Apostolic authority. But how can God "restore his everlasting gospel through living prophets"[43] who are themselves prone to error? What is the advantage of having doctrinal authority rest in the hands of fallible men who are prone to make mistakes? What benefit is there to be found in the errant words of modern man over that of the errant words of the ancients? With the belief that God's revelation to man can be defective, it is easy to see why Dr. Millet must affirm that "for the Latter-day Saints, the work of 'restoration' is a work in progress."[44]

It is significant that it is this Apostolic authority of the LDS Priesthood which Dr. Millet insists makes the LDS Church the one and only true church. It is their baptism that has authority. It is their teaching which can bring doctrinal correction. It is their efforts that have brought restoration to the church. It is their guidance which can preserve truth. "We hold to the truth that God has spoken anew in our day and restored his everlasting gospel through living prophets."[45] He quotes President Gordon B. Hinckley who put it this way:

The Lord said that this is the only true and living church upon the face of the earth with which He is well-pleased. I didn't say

---

40. Ibid., xiv.
41. Ibid., 50.
42. Ibid., 61.
43. Ibid., 64.
44. Ibid., 65.
45. Ibid., 64.

that. Those are His words. The Prophet Joseph was told that the other sects were wrong. Those are not my words. Those are the Lord's words. But *they are hard words for those of other faiths.*[46]

Once again, Dr. Millet's words are consistent with that of historic Mormonism. This book has brought great clarity to the question at hand. After reviewing this book it became readily apparent that, first, Mormonism is radically different from evangelical Christianity, and second, it has not undergone significant change.

Millet actually addresses this issue himself,

> The Church of Jesus Christ of Latter-day Saints has no inclination whatsoever toward ecumism and no desire to compromise one ounce of its doctrine or history in order to court favor among other religionists.[47]

President Gordon B. Hinckley avowed the same when he said in a 2001 conference, "Those who observe us say that we are moving into the mainstream of religion. We are not changing."[48]

Concluding Thoughts

Although there has been much that gives the appearance of being new, I believe that this brief review has pointed out that nothing significant has changed within Mormonism, other than a conscious effort and a deliberate plan to appear within the ranks of mainstream Christianity by using evangelical language. What is necessary as we communicate with our Mormon neighbors is that we define biblical words carefully, realizing that a failure to do so will result in misunderstanding. I think it is also abundantly clear that while there may be Mormons who are Christians, they are so, in spite of the clear teachings of Mormonism.

---

46. Ibid., 64. Quoting from Prophet Gordon B. Hinckley as recorded in *Ensign*, June 2004. Italics included in the original.

47. Taken from an article entitled, "Church Response to *Under the Banner of Heaven*. Http://www.lds.org/newsroom/mistakes.

48. Millet, *A Different Jesus?*, 141. Quoting *Ensign*, November 2001, p. 5.

PART TWO

The Bible and Mormon Teachings
A Comparison

"So often people of different religious persuasions simply talk past one another when they converse on matters religious. They may even use the same words, but they bring a different mindset and an entirely different perspective to the encounter."[1]

—Robert Millet

In this section, we will conduct a theological review covering the following issues: the scriptural rationale for a Christian to undergo such a project of examining Christianity and Mormonism; the contradictory beliefs of the Christian and the Mormon church; and an evaluation of whether or not (in light of these differences) Mormons should be classified as Christian.

---

1. Millet, *A Different Jesus?*, 172.

5

Scriptural Rationale

"Test everything. Hold on to the good."[1]

—The Apostle Paul

O NE OF the great dangers of comparing religious beliefs is that, if we are not careful, we can appear (or actually become) argumentative, boastful, arrogant, and brash. Well-intentioned Christians as well as Mormons have been guilty of mudslinging and name calling (or worse). As we begin this section, I would simply like to offer a word of caution from the Apostle Paul: "Knowledge puffs up, but love builds up" (1 Corinthians 8:1).[2]

The following material is presented out of love and concern from one who is on a journey for truth. It is not that I am right or have all the answers, but I do want what is right and believe God's Word contains those needed answers. Together, let us learn in an attitude of gentleness and grace. We should humbly and lovingly proceed on this journey for truth.

A Century 21 real estate commercial advertisement suggests that people don't care how much you know, unless they know how much you care. This is good advice in the arena of theology as well as business. We should always remember to present the truth in love.

---

1. 1 Thessalonians 5:21.

2. All Scripture has been quoted from the New International Version of the Bible (NIV).

At the same time, there will always be some who question the motives of those with even the purest intentions. Many have voiced suspicions as I've shown them the differences between Mormonism and Christianity. People often ask, "Why study Mor-monism, aren't they Christians too?" Or, "By attacking them, aren't you showing yourself to be un-Christian?" Or, (this is one of my favorites), "Does it really matter what you believe, as long as you are sincere?"

While I laugh (or groan) on the inside at such questions, I usually respond: "A close examination of Scripture will reveal that seeking truth and correct doctrine must be a priority for Christians." Notice the clear teaching of Jesus:

> Watch out for false prophets. They come to you in sheep's clothing, but inwardly they are ferocious wolves . . . Not everyone who says to me, 'Lord, Lord,' will enter the kingdom of heaven. (Matthew 7:15, 21)

It is a telling fact that almost every New Testament writer's words contain warnings about the dangers of false teaching and false teachers. Matthew writes, "Watch out that no one deceives you, for many will come in my name . . . and will deceive many" (Matthew 24:4–5). Luke writes, "Keep watch over yourselves and all the flock" (Acts 20:28). Peter warns: "There will be false teachers among you. They will secretly introduce destructive heresies, even denying the sovereign Lord who bought them" (2 Peter 2:1–3). Clearly, we are admonished to pay attention and correct those whose doctrine wanders.

John weighs in on the subject as well: "Dear friends, do not believe every spirit, but test the spirits to see whether they are from God, because many false prophets have gone out into the world" (1 John 4:1).

Of all the New Testament writers, Paul may have the most to say on the subject: "For such men are false apostles, deceitful workmen, masquerading as apostles of Christ. And no wonder, for Satan himself masquerades as an angel of light" (2 Corinthians 11:13–14). And:

> I am astonished that you are so quickly deserting the one who
> called you by the grace of Christ and are turning to a differ-
> ent gospel—which is really no gospel at all . . . But even if we
> or an angel from heaven should preach a gospel other than
> the one we preached to you, let him be eternally condemned.
> (Galatians 1:6–8)

Paul gives similar advice to his young apprentice, Timothy:
"Watch your life and doctrine closely. Persevere in them, because
if you do, you will save both yourself and your hearers" (1 Timothy
4:16). Paul's message is this: Proper doctrine is vitally important!

Clearly, we are told to evaluate teaching to make sure that
what is taught is true. We are repeatedly commanded to test teaching, correct doctrinal error, weigh what is taught, and discard as
falsehood those things which do not agree with the abiding word
of God. As you read these words, understand, this is not only true
when it comes to what others teach, but it is equally relevant to
what I present to you—test, evaluate, and keep only what is consistent with God's revealed Word.

Please realize, our purpose is not to criticize or attack, but
follow the scriptural admonition to watch doctrine closely.

What Is the Difference Anyway?

There is much debate about whether Mormonism should be classified as Christian.[3] This is an issue discussed at other places in this
work. At this point, we need only to affirm that Mormonism and
biblical Christianity differ greatly. While some might suggest that
Mormonism is moving closer to evangelical Christianity,[4] great di-
vergence can still be found on almost every major doctrine. What
is necessary is a willingness to give more than a cursory glance at
the surface of this topic.

---

3. This issue is discussed at great length in the chapter on literature review.
Note specifically discussions on books by Stephen E. Robinson and Robert L.
Millet.

4. See the literature review in chapter 2.

A major difficulty in studying Mormonism and Christianity stems from the fact that as dialogue occurs, the terminology used is the same, but the words are defined differently. Unless care is used in defining terms, these two faith systems may appear closer than they actually are. When we don't accurately define terms, we often talk past each other rather than to each other. Mormon author, Robert Millet recognizes this when he writes, "We use the same or similar words as our Christian neighbors to describe a Christian concept but discover upon more serious investigation that what we mean is at least slightly different."[5]

The purpose of this section, in part, is to demonstrate how different the definitions used really are. Before beginning, an assignment might prove useful. Take a moment and make a list of the most basic elements of your faith at the most elementary level. Once you have taken the time to do this, your list may include some or all of the following: God, Jesus, the Holy Spirit, man, sin, salvation, faith, the nature of Scripture, heaven, hell, the virgin birth, and creation. Mormonism and evangelical Christianity disagree on each of these—not small disagreements, but often views completely antithetical.

In the following chapters, we will examine basic elements of the Christian faith and perform the following tasks:

1) We will examine passages from the Bible.

2) We will examine Mormon literature[6] and writings.[7]

---

5. Robert Millet, *A Different Jesus?*, 81.

6. The Standard Works of the LDS church include the King James Version of the Bible as far as it is translated correctly; the Book of Mormon, which they hold to be a record of a Meso-American civilization inhabiting the America's between 600 B.C. and 421 A.D.; the Doctrine and Covenants, a recording of revelations from God given primarily to Joseph Smith, Jr; and the Pearl of Great Price, a collection of writings Mormons hold to be inspired published in the early days of the LDS Church.

7. To limit material to the Standard Works fails to take into account the evolutionary aspects of the LDS Church. Mormons also believe in Prophets, Seers and Revelators who cannot lead LDS people astray from God's will.

3) As accurately as possible, we will make observations about what we've read. Every effort has been made to not take passages out of context or quote obscure references.[8]

In presenting Mormon doctrine, it is necessary also to quote from Church authorities.

8. I have quoted only LDS sources in good standing with the LDS church.

6

God, the Bible, and Mormonism

*"The acceptance of modern and continuing revelation, including
the addition to the scriptural canon, is one of the distinctives of
Mormonism."*[1]

—Robert Millet

God in the Bible

THE BIBLE is not silent on the presence and nature of God. In
fact, its details are quite clear. In it you find there is only one
God. The three different persons of the Godhead are not only one
in purpose and thought, but they are one in essence and one in
their essential nature. God is only one being—there are not three
gods. Scripture is also clear about his attributes. These attributes
include, but are not limited to: his unchangeableness and eternality (Psalms 102:25–27); his omnipresence (Jeremiah 23:23–24;
Psalms 139:7–10); his omniscience (1 John 3:20); and his omnipo-
tence (Genesis 18:14; Jeremiah 32:27).

One of the most familiar passages in the Old Testament is often called the *Shema*: "Hear, O Israel: The Lord our God, the Lord
is one" (Deuteronomy 6:4). As you read the pages of the Bible, it
is made abundantly clear that God is one. "Know that the Lord
is God; besides him there is no other" (Deuteronomy 4:35). The
very idea that there are three gods to be worshiped rather than

---

1. Millet, *A Different Jesus?*, 15.

one is unthinkable. God alone is God and there is none like him. When he speaks, he alone is speaking. God is without beginning or end. To think that God came into existence, or that there are other gods beyond him is unimaginable. "Understand that I am he [God], before me no God was formed, nor will there be one after me" (Isaiah 43:10).

Isaiah 45:5 says, "I am the Lord, and there is no other. Apart from me there is no God." Isaiah 44:6–8 states, "I am the first and I am the last; apart from me there is no God." The psalmist records, "From everlasting to everlasting, you are God" (Psalms 90:2). The Bible records that God doesn't change (Malachi 3:6), he has no variation (James 1:17), and he alone possesses immortality (1 Timothy 6:16). You can read that God is spirit (John 4:24), and no man has seen him at any time (John 1:18). Paul speaks clearly to this issue when he says, "Now to the King eternal, immortal, invisible, the only God, be honor and glory forever and ever, Amen" (1 Timothy 1:17).

Observations about God and the Bible

From these and other passages from the Bible, it seems apparent that the Bible teaches that there is only one God. He is a spirit whom man has never seen, unchangeable, who has always existed, and who has always been and will always be God. But how do these teachings compare with Mormon doctrine?

God in Mormonism

Latter-day Saints also believe in God. But is the Mormon God the same as the Christian God? Here is a simple definition out of an LDS primer to help answer that question: "LDS belief is that he [God] is a glorified being who has attained eternal perfection in all things." The primer continues:

> The inspired words of Genesis states, "God created man in
> His own image, in the image of God created He him; male

and female created He them." If Genesis is to be taken literally, then God is in the image of man, and, therefore is a man
himself. That's the Latter-day Saint philosophy in a nutshell:
"Man is what God once was, God is what man may become"
(Joseph Smith, Jr.).[2] Members of the LDS Church believe they
can become like God himself.[3]

Although only a handbook and not an authoritative work of
the Mormon Church, this quotation accurately reflects historic
Mormon teaching.[4] Mormonism teaches that God was once a man
with a body, who attained perfection through spiritual progression. God traveled along a path all men can take, and because all
men can follow this path, there always have been and will continue
to be many Gods.[5] Mormon doctrine teaches that there are many
other Gods on many other worlds, yet LDS leaders insist they only
pray to one God.[6]

Notice some teachings from past Presidents, Prophets, and
Seers of the Church of Jesus Christ of Latter-day Saints. Joseph
Smith, founder and first President of the LDS Church records for
us, "There is one God for us . . . the head God of Gods . . ."[7] The
second President and Prophet of the Church, Brigham Young, who
served as such longer than any other President (30 years)[8] is re-

---

2. This saying is most often attributed to fifth President Lorenzo Snow.

3. Drew Williams, *Understanding Mormonism*, 14.

4. Drew Williams has taught LDS doctrine and essential gospel principles
at Brigham Young University for more than 16 years and continues to do so.

5. It is common LDS practice to capitalize "Gods" even when not referring
to "the God with whom we have to do." Out of respect for their beliefs, I have
made it a practice to capitalize all reference to God or Gods unless quoting
from a source that treats this differently.

6. Apostle Orson Hyde is quoted as saying, "But to our branch of the kingdom there is but one God, to whom we all owe the most perfect submission
and loyalty; yet our God is just as subject to still higher intelligneces, as we
should be to him" (See *Mormonism 101*, 35).

7. Joseph Smith, *Journal of Discourses*, 6:5.

8. Many within the Mormon church have wanted to distance themselves
from Brigham Young. I find this interesting in light of the fact that he was
God's prophet for them longer than any other.

corded as saying, "How many Gods are there, I do not know . . ."[9] Without meaning to be sarcastic, I'm confident this unknowable number was more than three. Orson Pratt gives clarity on this issue when he says, "In heaven there are many Gods . . . more Gods than there are particles of matter."[10]

Mormonism teaches that one may become a "God" through a series of progressive steps. God has not always been God, but there have always been Gods. B. H. Roberts stated:

> But if God the Father was not always God, but came to his present exalted position by degrees of progress as indicated in the teaching of the prophet, how has there been a God from all eternity? The answer is that there has been and there now exists an endless line of Divine Intelligences—Deities, stretching back into the eternities, that had no beginning and will have no end. Their existence runs parallel with endless duration, and their dominions are as limitless as boundless space.[11]

LDS Church historians and authors have consistently affirmed a belief in multiple, generational Gods. What is meant by generational Gods? Heber Kimball explains, "God is connected to a God farther back . . . and there is one before him."[12] Mormonism teaches that God had a father, who had a father before him in an endless succession. A familiar argument commonly used by Mormons states simply, "If there is a father, there must also be a grandfather." There are also many references to a heavenly mother and heavenly parents.[13]

---

9. Brigham Young, *Journal of Discourses*, 7:333.

10. Orson Pratt, *Journal of Discourses*, 2:345 and *The Seer*, 37, 132.

11. B. H. Roberts, *New Witnesses for God*, vol. 1, 461.

12. Heber Kimball, *Journal of Discourses*, 5:19; 8:2111.

13. One current LDS training manual states, "Our Father in heaven was once a man as we are now capable of physical death. By obedience to eternal gospel principles he progressed from one stage of life to another until he attained the state that we call exaltation or godhood. In such a condition, he and our mother in heaven were empowered to give birth to spirit children whose potential was equal to that of their heavenly parents. We are those spirit children" (*Achieving a Celestial Marriage*, 132).

Almost every LDS family has a lexicon of Mormon theology that they use as a reference guide. If a Mormon has a question about general Church practice or philosophy about a particular subject, they are encouraged to consult the Mormon historian, Bruce McConkie.[14] He writes the following: "There are three Gods we worship, but an infinite number of Gods."[15]

Far from the biblical doctrine of God being one, Mormonism teaches that there are not only three Gods with whom they concern themselves, but an infinite number of Gods. Not only does Mormonism unwaveringly teach there are three separate, distinct Gods they worship, they also believe that God has a body. "God is in form, like a man with body and voice."[16]

> The personality of the Godhead is an absolute doctrine of the Church regarding which there can be no doubt or controversy. The Father, the Son, and the Holy Ghost are three separate and distinct personages; the first two with glorified tabernacles [bodies] of flesh and bone, the third a personage of spirit.[17]

The Doctrine and Covenants (D&C),[18] one of the standard works of the Mormon Church, makes this clear. "God the Father has a glorified, exalted body; the Father has a body of flesh and bones as tangible as man's" (D&C 130:22).[19] This only confirms what Joseph Smith taught, "See him like a man in form, as a very man."[20]

Mormon literature is replete with examples of this teaching. "Let me tell you how God came to be a God, he was once a man like us."[21] Orson Pratt writes, "The Gods were once all in a fallen

14. Drew Williams, *Understanding Mormonism*, 293.

15. Bruce McConkie, *Mormon Doctrine*, 322, 576–77.

16. *Principles of the Gospel*, 193–94.

17. *Principles of the Gospel*, 182.

18. The standard abbreviation for the Doctrine and Covenants is D&C in Mormon writings.

19. Another Standard Work, the Pearl of Great Price, says, "In the image of His own body, He created them" (Book of Moses 2:27).

20. Joseph Smith, *Journal of Discourses*, 6:3.

21. Ibid.

state . . . but have been exalted."[22] Brigham Young affirms, "God was once a mortal as we are . . . we were created to become Gods."[23] Milton Hunter puts it quite succinctly, "God was once a mortal man."[24] The founder and first Prophet, Joseph Smith, even records for us, "We have imagined and supposed that God was God from all eternity. I will refute that idea, and take away the veil, so that you can see."[25] This whole idea of God being mortal and living in a fallen state suggests that at one time God himself was not, nor is he now, perfect. The God of Mormonism is continually progressing.

Observations about God in Mormonism

These references from Mormon literature reveal numerous differences regarding the Mormon God and the God of biblical Christianity. In Mormonism: there are many Gods—too numerous to count; God has not always been God—God changes; and God dwells within a mortal body. In addition, we have learned that the Mormon God is not, nor will he necessarily ever be, perfect.

Through the use of the biblical text and Mormon literature, the corresponding views of God have been compared. At this point, three simple questions need to be asked:

1. When it comes to a biblical view and the Mormon view of God as contained in their literature, are there differences?

2. If there are differences, are these differences significant?

3. Without having to state which position is "right," or "wrong," are we justified in saying, at least at this one particular point, Christianity and Mormonism are not the same?

---

22. Orson Pratt, The Seer, 23.

23. Brigham Young, Journal of Discourses, 7:333.

24. Milton Hunter, The Gospel through the Ages, 104.

25. Joseph Smith, Documented History of the Church of Jesus Christ of Latter-day Saints, 6:304.

It seems apparent that one must conclude that while the God of the Bible is one, eternal,[26] omnipotent, omnipresent, and never changes; the God of Mormonism has not always existed as God, he has and continues to develop as God, and due to the fact that he is constrained by a physical body—is limited in both time and space. Although Mormons will and do argue that they only have dealings with one God, from their writings it appears he is a different God than the Bible describes.

---

26. Mormons believe that everything is eternal in the sense that everything has always existed in a preexistent state. Therefore, they would argue God is eternal, but that he hasn't existed as God for eternity. Robert Millet goes one step further and argues that Mormons do believe that God is eternal, but he redefines eternity as a long time. For more information on this, see chapter 2.

7

Jesus, the Bible, and Mormonism

"Don't Mormons believe that Jesus and the devil are brothers?"[1]

—Mike Huckabee

"What do I believe about Jesus Christ? I believe that Jesus Christ is the son of God and the savior of mankind. My church's beliefs about Christ may not all be the same as those of other faiths. Each religion has its own unique doctrines and history."[2]

—Mitt Romney

Jesus in the Bible

THE BIBLICAL picture of Jesus is that he is fully God, who emptied himself of his divine nature and temporarily became man through the incarnation (Philippians 2:5–8). In his pre-incarnate state, he possessed all the attributes of God, but through a process of self-limitation, he became man (Hebrews 2:17).[3] To understand the Jesus of the Bible, you must understand him to be both fully God and fully man. Christianity presents this model: Jesus—God from the beginning, who emptied himself to live as a man, who after the death, burial, and resurrection, was exalted back to his rightful position.

---

1. The Associated Press as reported by Fox News, December 12, 2007.

2. The Associated Press, December 6, 2007.

3. I like to speak of Jesus coming to earth and leaving his power-tools at home.

Once again, let's look at the clear teachings of Scripture. Jesus existed as the Creator of all things before the beginning of time showing that he is uncreated. John 1:1, 14 tells us that Jesus was God from the beginning and was involved in the creation process.

> In the beginning was the Word, and the Word was with God, and the Word was God. He was with God in the beginning. Through him all things were made; without him nothing was made that has been made... The Word became flesh and made his dwelling among us. We have seen his glory, the glory of the One and Only, who came from the father, full of grace and truth.

Colossians 1:16–17 tells us:

> For by him all things were created: things in heaven and on earth, visible and invisible, whether thrones or powers or rulers or authorities; all things were created by him and for him. He is before all things, and in him all things hold together.

Jesus is the exact representation of God. "The Son is the radiance of God's glory and the exact representation of his being, sustaining all things by his powerful word" (Hebrews 1:3).

Jesus is the unique and only Son of God. "For God so loved the world that he gave his one and only Son, that whoever believes in him shall not perish but have eternal life" (John 3:16).[4]

Jesus was born of a virgin, yet called God. "The virgin will be with child and will give birth to a son, and they will call him Immanuel—which means, 'God with us'" (Matthew 1:23). "For to us a child is born, to us a son is given, and the government will be on his shoulders. And he will be called Wonderful Counselor, Mighty God, Everlasting Father, Prince of Peace" (Isaiah 9:6).

Observations about Jesus and the Bible

Notice from these and other passages[5] that Jesus has existed from eternity as the "only one of a kind" Son of God. He was born of a

---

4. In Greek, "*monogenos*"—the only one of a kind.

5. Here are more passages that teach that Jesus shares the nature of God.

virgin as God incarnate (God become man). Jesus is unlike any other human that has ever lived, not only because of his sinless life, but because of his timeless past.

Jesus in Mormonism

Far from being eternally God, Latter-day Saints believe that Jesus progressed to become God of this earth.[6] Before becoming a man, he was first conceived as a spirit child in heaven among countless others. Later, when he came to earth, he became the literal Son of God.[7] In Mormonism, Elohim (Father God) and Jehovah (Jesus) are not only two distinct people,[8] but Jehovah is the direct offspring of Elohim and is just one of many. Jesus "was the first spirit child of Elohim, of which there are countless others."[9] "Jesus Christ is the spiritual and physical Son of the Father."[10] Bruce McConkie writes:

> All men (Christ included) were born as the sons of God in the spirit, one man (Christ only) was born as the Son of God in the mortal world. He is the only begotten in the flesh. God was his Father; Mary was his mother. His Father was an immortal man; his mother a mortal woman. He is the Son of God in the same literal, full, and complete sense in which he is the Son of Mary. There is nothing symbolic or figurative about it.[11]

John 8:58; 10:30–38; 20:28; Acts 20:28; Romans 9:5; Titus 2:13; 2 Peter 1:1; Matthew 28:19–20.

6. As the . . . foreordained Redeemer of this world, Jesus Christ became the God of this world" (*Principles of the Gospel*, 196).

7. In chapter two, I cited Robinson as saying that Jesus had forty-six chromosomes—one strand from his mother and one strand from his father. Millet also declared that Jesus was the literal son of God and not just the son of God in some metaphorical sense.

8. This poses a problem for Mormon theology as the Bible uses the two names together frequently in Scripture. For example, Moses declared, "Hear, O Israel: The Lord [Jehovah] our God [Elohim] the Lord is one" (Deut 6:4).

9. *Principles of the Gospel*, 201.

10. Ibid., 196.

11. Bruce McConkie, *A New Witness for the Articles of Faith*, 67.

Brigham Young said it this way: "The birth of the Savior was as natural as are the births of our children; it was the result of natural action. He . . . was begotten of his Father, as we were our fathers."[12] Heber C. Kimball concurs, "According to the Scriptures, he is the first begotten of his father in the flesh, and there was nothing unnatural about it."[13] Brigham Young stated emphatically, "Now, remember from this time forth, and forever, that Jesus Christ was not begotten by the Holy Ghost."[14] Apostle James Talmage writes:

> Jesus Christ is the Son of Elohim both as spiritual and bodily offspring; that is to say Elohim is literally the Father of the spirit of Jesus Christ and also of the body in which Jesus Christ performed His mission in the flesh.[15]

In Mormonism, Jesus is eternal, only in the sense that he was alive in a preexistent state before he came to earth. Bruce McConkie writes:

> Implicit in his [Jesus] spirit birth as the Firstborn is the fact that, as with all the spirit children of the Father, he had a beginning; there was a day when he came into being as a conscious identity, as a spirit entity, as an organized intelligence . . . How is he [Jesus] the Eternal One? It might be said that he is eternal, as all men are, meaning that spirit element—the intelligence which was organized into intelligences—has always existed and is therefore eternal.[16]

As a noble spirit child, Mormonism teaches that Jesus became the God of this world.

> In the council in heaven during our pre-mortal existence he was chosen and ordained to be the Redeemer of our sins . . . Jesus Christ became the God of this world . . . [His becoming] God of this earth was clearly explained when he as the risen

---

12. *Journal of Discourses*, 8:211.

13. Ibid.

14. Ibid., 1:51.

15. James Talmage, *Articles of Faith*, 466.

16. Bruce McConkie, *The Promised Messiah*, 165.

> Lord, following his crucifixion and resurrection, appeared to his people in the land Bountiful on this continent.[17]

Interestingly enough, even the ordination of Jesus to become God of this world shows that Jesus was not unique. At least one other child of God vied for the position of Savior. Milton Hunter writes, "The appointment of Jesus to be the Savior of the world was contested by one of the other sons of God. He was called Lucifer, son of the morning . . . this spirit-brother of Jesus desperately tried to become the Savior of mankind."[18] Jesus was not unique in the spirit world, nor does he remain unique. Sixth Prophet of the Church, Joseph F. Smith said boldly that "the day will come—and it is not far distant, when the name of the Prophet Joseph Smith will be coupled with the name of Jesus Christ of Nazareth."

Observations about Jesus in Mormonism

While there is no doubt that LDS members claim Jesus Christ is the central figure in their theology and daily living, there appears to be some distinguishing characteristics in Mormon thought. To summarize, the Mormon Jesus is not a "one of a kind" being in a traditionally Christian sense, nor is he the only Son of God. In the spirit world, all people were brothers of Jesus and sons and daughters of God. In this prior existence, Jesus was elected by a council of Gods to become Savior. In order to accomplish salvation, he became a physical man by being sired by a God of flesh and blood. Later, after living life on earth, Jesus became God. Although eternally existent as a spirit child, Jesus has not been eternally God. Jesus progressed to godhood in a manner we can follow.

So we again must ask:

1. When it comes to a biblical view of Jesus and the Mormon view of Jesus as contained in Mormon literature, are there differences?

---

17. *Principles of the Gospel*, 196.

18. Milton Hunter, *Gospel Through the Ages*, 15.

Listen to the words of the late Prophet and President of the Mormon Church, Gordon B. Hinkley, in his address to the General Conference on April 2002.

> As a church, we have critics—many of them. They say we do not believe in the traditional Christ of Christianity. There is some substance to what they say. Our faith, our knowledge, is not based on ancient tradition—our faith, our knowledge comes of the witness of a prophet in this dispensation.[19]

Even such an authority as the President of the Mormon church has acknowledged the differences.

Still we must ask:

2. Are these differences significant? And,

3. Without having to state which position is "right," or "wrong," are we justified in saying, at least at this one particular point, Christianity and Mormonism are not the same?

We must conclude that while the Jesus of the Bible is the eternally existent creator of heaven and earth who emptied himself and came to earth to live temporarily as a man; the Jesus of Mormonism, while eternally existent as a spirit entity, first became a man who then developed into God. Although Mormons will and do argue that they worship the same Jesus, it must be admitted that there are significant differences.

---

19. Gordon B. Hinkley, April 2002, General Conference.

8

The Holy Spirit, the Bible, and Mormonism

*"The Godhead is the divine council of three separate and distinct
personages, often referred to as the Holy Trinity. The Godhead is
comprised of Elohim (the Father), Jehovah (Jesus), and the Holy
Ghost. Both the Father and Jesus have had physical bodies, the
Holy Ghost has not yet descended to a state of mortality."*[1]

—Drew Williams

The Holy Spirit and the Bible

THE BIBLE clearly says that the Holy Spirit is a non-corporeal, personal being with intellect, emotions, and will.[2] Biblically, the Holy Spirit is not described as simply a spiritual presence, he is described as being fully God (2 Samuel 23:2–3; Acts 5:1–4; 1 Corinthians 6:19–20). He shares the same attributes as God and Jesus and yet is distinguished from them. The Holy Spirit is a person and he possesses characteristics that define personhood, including, but not limited to: knowledge (1 Corinthians 2:10–11), emotion (Ephesians 4:30), love (Romans 15:30), will (1 Corinthians 12:11), and mind (Romans 8:27).

Not only is the Holy Spirit referred to in Scripture as God, but he also shares the noncommunicable attributes of God: he is

---

1. Drew Williams, *Understanding Mormonism*, 15.
2. See John 16:5–16.

omnipresent (Psalms 139:7–10); omnipotent (Luke 1:35–37); omniscient (Isaiah 40:13); and eternal (Hebrews 9:14).[3]

Observations about the Holy Spirit and the Bible

The Father, Son, and Holy Spirit, biblically are not separate Gods, but are distinct persons within the one triune Godhead. The Bible teaches that they are distinct, yet are only one God.[4]

The Holy Spirit and Mormonism

In the LDS *Articles of Faith*, it says, "We believe in God, the Eternal Father, and in His Son, Jesus Christ, and in the Holy Ghost."[5] This sounds much like evangelical Christianity until you understand that the Father, Son, and Holy Spirit are totally separate Gods.

> Three separate personages—Father, Son, and Holy Ghost—comprise the Godhead. As each of these persons is a God, it is evident, from this standpoint alone, that a plurality of Gods exists. To us, speaking in the proper finite sense, these three are the only Gods we worship. But in addition there is an infinite number of holy personages, drawn from the worlds without number, who have passed on to exaltation and are thus Gods.[6]

In Mormonism, the Godhead is the divine council of three separate and distinct personages: Elohim (the Father); Jehovah (Jesus); and the Holy Ghost. Both the Father and Jesus have physical bodies, the Holy Ghost has not yet descended to a state of mortality.[7] The Doctrine and Covenants records, "The Father has

---

3. Compare Psalms 95:7–11 with Hebrews 3:7–19; Isaiah 6:8–10 with Acts 28:25; Jeremiah 31:33–34 with Hebrews 10:15–16.

4. For more scriptural references see: Matthew 28:19; Mark 3:28–29; John 14:26; 16:7–14; Acts 5:3–4; Romans 15:30; 1 Corinthians 2:10–13; 12:11; and Ephesians 4:30.

5. Article 1 of the *Articles of Faith* which is contained in the Doctrine and Covenants.

6. Bruce McConkie, *Mormon Doctrine*, 576–77.

7. Drew Williams, *Understanding Mormonism*, 15. This is interesting!

a body of flesh and bones as tangible as man's; the Son also; but the Holy Ghost has not a body of flesh and bones, but is a personage of Spirit" (D&C 130:22). Mormon scholar Robert L. Millet writes, "The Godhead consists of three distinct personages and three Gods—the Father, Son, and Holy Spirit. The Father and Son have bodies of flesh and bones, while the Holy Spirit is a spirit personage."[8]

Observations about the Holy Spirit and Mormonism

While evangelical Christianity views the Holy Spirit as part of a monotheistic Godhead, Mormonism teaches that the Holy Spirit is a separate and unique God. Joseph Fielding Smith wrote, "Many men say there is one God; the Father, the Son and the Holy Ghost are only one God. I say that is a strange God anyhow—three in one, and one in three . . . All are to be crammed into one God . . . he would be a giant or a monster."[9]

At this point, things get a bit dicey. In some Mormon writings, there appears to be a difference between the Holy Ghost and the Holy Spirit.[10] The tenth Prophet of the Church, Joseph Fielding Smith wrote;

> The Holy Ghost should not be confused with the Spirit which fills the immensity of space and which is everywhere present. This other spirit [The Holy Spirit] is impersonal and has no size, nor dimension; it proceeds forth from the presence of the Father and the Son and is in all things. We should speak of the

---

According to Mormon theology, eternal progression requires the obtaining of a physical body to obtain Godhood. The Holy Spirit does not meet their own criteria, but is still to be considered one of their Gods.

8. Robert Millet, *A Different Jesus?*, 198.

9. Smith, *Teachings of the Prophet Joseph Smith*, 349.

10. See Joseph McConkie, *Encyclopedia of Mormonism*, 2:649; LeGrand Richards, *A Marvelous Work and Wonder*, 117; and Joseph Smith, *Improvement Era*, 389.

Holy Ghost as a personage and 'he' and this other spirit [The Holy Spirit] as "it."[11]

Bruce McConkie concurs:

The Holy Ghost . . . can be in only one place at one time, and he does not and cannot transform himself into any other form or image other than that of the Man whom he is . . . The Holy Spirit is a Spirit Personage . . . he has power to perform unique functions for men.[12]

When this distinction is made between the Holy Ghost and the Holy Spirit, the Holy Ghost is viewed as a spirit-child, born of heavenly parents, and has the shape of a man. The Holy Ghost can only be in one location at a time, and is one of the three Gods of this earth. In contrast, the Holy Spirit is a divine eminence or influence that can be felt universally among Mormons and helps them bear witness to the truths of Mormonism. This doctrine, while not infrequently taught, appears to be more pronounced in early Mormonism and is the source of much ambiguity and inconsistency.[13] Of course, biblically, Holy Spirit and Holy Ghost are simply two different English translations of the Greek phrase *"agios pneumos"*—with the King James Version opting to use the phrase, "Holy Ghost" while other English versions choose the "Holy Spirit."

This brings me once again to our questions:

1. When it comes to a biblical view of the Holy Spirit and the Mormon view as contained in Mormon literature, are there differences?

2. If there are differences, are these differences significant?

---

11. Joseph Fielding Smith, *Doctrines of Salvation*, 1:50.

12. Bruce McConkie, *Mormon Doctrine*, 359.

13. According to Mormon theology, eternal progression requires the obtaining of a physical body to obtain Godhood. The Holy Spirit does not meet their criteria, yet is still considered to be one of their Gods.

3. Without having to state which position is "right," or "wrong," are we justified in saying, at least at this one particular point, Christianity and Mormonism are not the same?

We must conclude that the Holy Spirit of the Bible is different from the Holy Spirit described in Mormonism. Although the same nomenclature is used, there are significant differences.

9

Premortal Existence, Man, and Sin

"From a Latter-day Saint perspective, humankind did not suddenly spring into existence at the time of their mortal birth. We have always lived."[1]

—Robert Millet

The Bible: Premortal Existence, Man, and Sin

THE BIBLE teaches that God is the creator of the heavens and earth. He alone created the universe and no one else existed to help. Isaiah records God's words for us:

> This is what the Lord says—your Redeemer, who formed you in the womb: I am the Lord, who has made all things, who alone stretched out the heavens, who spread out the earth by myself . . . I am the Lord, and there is no other; apart from me there is no God . . . It is I who made the earth and created mankind upon it. (Isaiah 44:24; 45:5, 12)

The Bible tells us that man is not God, but a creation of God. We learn in the opening pages of the Bible that man is a finite being, not an eternal one. The first man was created at a specific point in time (Genesis 1:27; 2:7, 21–22) and did not exist when God was creating the universe (Job 38:4).[2] The Psalmist writes,

---

1. Millet, *A Different Jesus?*, 18.

2. In this passage, God asks a rhetorical question of Job, "Where were you when I laid the earth's foundation?"

"You made him [man] a little lower than the heavenly beings" and this caused David to ask, "What is man that you are mindful of him?" (Psalms 8:4–5).

Although Scripture acknowledges that God knew man before he was born,[3] the emphasis is on what God knew,[4] not that man was eternally preexistent. Throughout Scripture, we are told that the body and soul of each person is formed in the womb.[5]

We are also taught in Scripture that the first ploy of Satan in the garden was telling Eve that man could become like God.

> Now the serpent was more crafty than any of the wild animals the Lord God had made. He said to the woman, "Did God really say, 'You must not eat from any tree in the garden'?" The woman said to the serpent, "We may eat from the trees in the garden, but God did say, 'You must not eat from the tree that is in the middle of the garden, and you must not touch it, or you will die.'" "You will not surely die," the serpent said to the woman. "For God knows that when you eat of it your eyes will be opened, and you will be like God." (Genesis 3:1–5)

Although man was created to be with God, he was not created to be God. Also, we learn that man severed his relationship with God when he sinned in the garden. The disobedience of Adam and Eve was a great evil and through their actions, sin entered the world. Man's sin in the garden not only caused him to be separated from God (Genesis 3:14–19; Romans 5:12; Psalms 51:5), but sin brought death (Romans 6:23) and death spread to all men, because all men sin. The universal problem of humanity is that all, like Adam and Eve, have sinned. Consequently, all will be judged for the sins they commit, and those found guilty of their sin will be worthy of death (Romans 3:23; 6:23).

---

3. Jeremiah 1:5 says, "Before I formed you in the womb I knew you, before you were born I set you apart."

4. Paul tells us that God is able to call those "things that are not as though they were" (Romans 4:17).

5. See Psalms 119:73; 139:13–16; Job 10:8–12; 31:15; Zechariah 12:1.

Mormonism: Premortal Existence, Man, and Sin

Mormonism varies greatly from Christianity at each of the above points. Unlike the biblical view, Mormonism does not believe that human life begins with conception in the womb,[6] but rather it teaches that everything (including man) has eternally existed in a world before our own.

> The doctrine has prevailed that matter was created out of nothing, but the Lord declares that the elements are eternal. Matter always did and . . . always will exist. . . . We discover . . . that the intelligent part of man was not created, but always existed. It is expressed in several revelations, that man was in the beginning with God . . . however, man was a spirit unembodied.[7]

Current Brigham Young University professor, Drew Williams writes,

> We existed in God's presence long before we showed up on the earth. During the time we walked and talked while in the presence of God, mankind developed characteristics at the individual level. Some spirits rose in stature and responsibility, others focused on their own personal agendas—pretty much the same way man has developed throughout mortal history. However, there is one important difference. As premortal spirits, man was not capable of *experiencing* the actual emotions and choices an unbridled life has to offer. In a way, our pre-earth existence was all about research, and not about hands-on application. At some point in progress, as the human race developed . . . God decided it was time for his children to get a chance to experience life firsthand. It was time to be tested, time to *leave the nest*.[8]

---

6. "The intelligence of spirits had no beginning, neither will it have an end" (*Teachings of the Prophet Joseph Smith*, 353). "Our Father in Heaven begat all the spirits that ever were, or ever will be, upon this earth; and they were born spirits in the eternal world" (*Discourses of Brigham Young*, 24).

7. Joseph Fielding Smith, *Church History and Modern Revelation*, 1:401. See also Book of Moses chapter 3 and Book of Abraham chapter 3 in Pearl of Great Price.

8. Drew Williams, *Understanding Mormonism*, 22. Italics included in the original.

Mormon Scholar Robert Millet confirms this belief when he writes,

> Latter-day Saints believe that men and women are the spirit sons and daughters of God, that we lived in a premortal existence before birth . . . Thus God is literally our spirit Father, and we inherit from him divine qualities and attributes. In the long expanse of time before we were born into mortality, the spirit sons and daughters of God developed talents, strengths, and capacities.[9]

Mormonism clearly teaches that man eternally existed before he came to earth.[10] But the difference between Christianity and Mormonism runs much deeper. In Mormon doctrine, not only has man always existed, but men were designed to become Gods. Robert Millet quotes LDS President Gordon B. Hinckley as saying, "the whole design of the gospel is to lead us onward and upward to greater achievement, even, eventually to Godhood."[11] Joseph Fielding Smith said, "The promises are made to us, that we may be made like him."[12] But what exactly is meant by the phrase, "be made like him?" Mormon handbooks bring clarity to this issue:

> Man has within him the power . . . that eventually he shall become like the Father and the Son . . . then shall they be gods, because they have no end; therefore shall they be from everlasting to everlasting . . . then they shall become Gods.[13]

While some assert that this only suggests that man will become like God,[14] this is not the case. Brigham Young said, "Man

---

9. Robert Millet, *A Different Jesus?*, 19.

10. "Where did we come from? From God. Our spirits existed before they came to this World. They were in the council of the heavens before the foundations of the earth were laid" (President Joseph F. Smith, *Gospel Doctrine*, 93).

11. Robert Millet, *A Different Jesus?*, 117.

12. Joseph Fielding Smith, *Doctrine of Salvation*, 1:10.

13. *Principles of the Gospel*, 160–62.

14. Robert Millet writes, "While Latter-day Saints certainly accept the teachings of Joseph Smith regarding man becoming like God, we do not fully comprehend all that is entailed by such a bold declaration. Subsequent or even

is God in embryo."[15] Prophet and founder of the church, Joseph Smith said, "We can become Gods and pass by the Gods."[16]

This is not a fringe teaching held by only a few. James Talmage taught, "God progressed by a path his children can follow."[17] Apostle John Widtsoe said, "God and man are of the same race, differing only in their degrees of advancement."[18] President John Taylor concurs, "We look at him [man] as emanating from the Gods—as a God in embryo—as an eternal being who had an existence before he came here."[19] Brigham Young said, "The intelligence we possess is from our Father and our God. Every attribute that is in His character is in His children in embryo."[20] Heber C. Kimball writes, "When you have learned to become obedient . . . You become qualified, and capable, and capacitated to become a father of an earth yourselves."[21]

> The stunning truth, lost to humankind before the Restoration, is that each of us is a god in embryo. We may become as our heavenly parents. We, too, in exalted families, may one day preside in our own realms.[22]

As radical a departure as spiritual progression to Godhood seems from a biblical perspective, the differences run deeper still. Even the nature of sin itself has been redefined by Mormonism. Unlike the Bible, Mormonism does not teach that Adam and Eve sinned in the garden but that they merely disobeyed God's

---

current Church leaders have spoken very little concerning which of God's attributes are communicable and which are incommunicable." *A Different Jesus?*, 117.

15. Brigham Young, *Journal of Discourses*, 3:93; 10:233; 4:271.

16. Joseph Smith, *Doctrine and Covenants*, 132:19–20.

17. James Talmage, *Articles of Faith*, 430.

18. Milton Hunter, *The Gospel through the Ages*, 107.

19. *Journal of Discourses*, 8:1.

20. Ibid., 12:105.

21. Ibid., 1:356.

22. *Ensign*, June 1993, 10.

command. "Adam didn't sin in the garden, but chose the lesser of two evils."[23] President Joseph F. Smith said:

> I never speak of the part Eve took in this fall as a sin, nor do I accuse Adam of a sin. It is true, the Lord warned Adam and Eve that to partake of the fruit they would transgress a law, and this happened. But it is not always a sin to transgress a law ... That is, his transgression was in accordance with law.[24]

Sterling Still, Assistant to the Apostles, is recorded as saying, "Adam fell, but he fell in the right direction. He fell toward the goal. Adam fell, but he fell upward."[25] Sin, rather than being defined as breaking God's law, is defined as doing anything that hinders our spiritual progression to Godhood. Mormonism actually teaches that the "Fall" of Adam and Eve in Genesis was actually a blessed event. It was the fruit in the garden that set in motion the plan of eternal progression.

> If Adam had not eaten of the forbidden fruit ... he and Eve would also have remained unable to bring other spirits into the world as their children. If Adam had not transgressed [broken the law] he would not have fallen ... And they would have had no children (2 Nephi 2:22–23). Thus, the purpose of this earth's creation would have been frustrated. Unless he broke the commandment not to eat the fruit, Adam could not have fulfilled the commandment to multiply and replenish the earth, to bring more of the Father's children to the earth. Adam was given two commandments that seemed to oppose each other so that he could use his free agency ... By partaking of the forbidden fruit, Adam was able to obey the commandment to bring forth children, and he also made it possible for us to fulfill our purpose on earth to learn through our experiences the good from the evil: "And now, behold, if Adam had not transgressed he would not have fallen ... : wherefore they would have remained in a state of innocence, having no joy,

---

23. *Principles of the Gospel*, 167.

24. *Doctrines of Salvation*, 1:114.

25. *Deseret News*, 31 July 1965.

for they knew no misery; doing no good, for they knew no sin." (2 Nephi 2:22–23)[26]

The Book of Moses in The Pearl of Great Price records:

> And Eve, his wife, heard all these things and was glad saying: "Were it not for our transgression we never should have had seed [children], and never should have known good and evil, and the joy of our redemption, and the eternal life which God giveth unto all the obedient." (Moses 5:11)

Robert Millet writes, "Latter-day Saints believe in a 'fortunate fall,' that the fall of our first parents was as much part of the plan of God as the Atonement."[27]

Observations about Man and Sin in Mormonism

In Mormonism, man preexisted as organized intelligences before Spirit heaven. These intelligences entered Spirit bodies by way of heavenly parents who gave them spiritual bodies. Progression to Godhood includes a probationary time here on earth which was made possible when Adam transgressed in the garden. This transgression of God's command provided the opportunity for advancement and enabled Adam and Eve to have physical children.[28] The ultimate goal of life on earth is to progress and to eventually become a perfected God. Sin, thus, can be defined as anything that hinders man's spiritual progression to Godhood.

Questions:

1. When it comes to a biblical view of premortal existence, man, sin, and the Mormon view as contained in Mormon literature, are there differences?

2. If there are differences, are these differences significant?

---

26. *Principles of the Gospel*, 167. Brackets included in original.

27. Robert Millet, *A Different Jesus?*, 84.

28. "By partaking of the forbidden fruit, Adam was able to obey the commandment to bring forth children" (*Principles of the Gospel*, 167).

3. Without having to state which position is "right," or "wrong," are we justified in saying, at least at this one particular point, Christianity and Mormonism are not the same?

We must conclude that the nature of man and the essence of sin portrayed in the Bible is much different from that portrayed in Mormon literature. One must admit that there are significant differences.

10

Salvation

"It requires all the atonement of Christ, the mercy of the Father, the pity of angels and the grace of the Lord Jesus Christ to be with us always, and then to do the very best we possibly can, to get rid of this sin within us, so that we may escape from this world into the celestial kingdom."[1]

—Robert Millet

The Bible and Salvation

THE BIBLICAL picture of salvation is truly good news! Although man has alienated himself from God (Romans 3:23), God loved us so much that he sent his son to pay the penalty for our sin (John 3:16). Christ was able to be the perfect sacrifice because he was sinless (2 Corinthians 5:21; Hebrews 4:15; 7:26) and through his death on the cross (1 Peter 2:24), was able to take upon himself the full penalty of our sins (Galatians 3:13). His atonement is able to provide for all sins for all time and is available to all (1 John 2:2). God offers this salvation freely as a gift and it is not accomplished by human effort. "For it is by grace you have been saved, through faith—not from yourselves, it is the gift of God—not by works, so that no one can boast" (Ephesians 2:8–9). "Salvation is found in no one else, for there is no other name under heaven given to men by which we must be saved" (Acts 4:12). It is only through Christ

---

1. Millet, *A Different Jesus?*, 88.

that our sins can be forgiven (1 John 1:9) and we can be declared "not guilty" (Romans 3:24; 5:1). As Christians, we are set apart for service to God (1 Corinthians 1:2; 1 Thessalonians 5:23). The gospel message is that although we were sinners and enemies of God, Christ died for us (Romans 5:8–11) and thereby reconciled us to God. One of the most powerful descriptions of salvation can be found in the writings of the Apostle Paul.

> At one time we too were foolish, disobedient, deceived and enslaved by all kinds of passions and pleasures. We lived in malice and envy, being hated and hating one another. But when the kindness and love of God our Savior appeared, he saved us, not because of righteous things we had done, but because of his mercy. He saved us through the washing of rebirth and renewal by the Holy Spirit, whom he poured out on us generously through Jesus Christ our Savior, so that having been justified by his grace, we might become heirs having the hope of eternal life." (Titus 3:3–7)

Observations about Biblical Salvation

Biblically, it seems apparent that we are saved by the grace of God through faith and that there is nothing that a person can do to save themselves. Salvation is only available through Jesus Christ, having been purchased by his death on the cross. It is only through Christ's death, burial, and resurrection that humanity has hope.

Mormonism and Salvation

In Mormonism, one needs to make the distinction between general salvation and individual salvation before addressing this topic.

> In The Church of Jesus Christ of Latter-day Saints, the term *salvation* is used in two ways. In its general sense, salvation will be given to all men (except the sons of perdition) because Christ broke the bands of death and bore the sins of the world (see D&C 76:40–48). *Salvation* is also used in the Church to mean exaltation in the celestial kingdom. This type of salva-

tion comes only to those who accept and obey all the laws and ordinances of the gospel.[2]

Robert Millet writes:

> Here, as in other theological matters, we use the same or similar words as our Christian neighbors to describe a Christian concept but discover upon more serious investigation that what we mean is at least slightly different . . . From an LDS perspective, there are two types of salvation . . . universal and individual. All who take a physical body—good or bad, evil or righteous—will be resurrected . . . This is universal salvation. It is salvation from physical death, a salvation available to all . . . Individual salvation is another matter. Though all salvation [universal] is available through the goodness and grace of Christ, there are certain things that must be done in order for divine grace and mercy to be activated in the lives of individual followers of the Christ [individual salvation].[3]

Robert Millet gives more details later when he writes:

> Universal salvation is from physical death, a salvation available to all. *Immortality* is salvation from the grave . . . it is a universal gift. Individual salvation is another matter. Though all salvation is available through the goodness and grace of Christ, there are certain things that must be done in order for divine grace and mercy to be activated.[4]

While Mormonism does believe that Christ's sacrifice provides the opportunity for all to be resurrected from the grave,[5] true salvation is defined in terms of exaltation. "Salvation is used in the Church to mean exaltation in the celestial kingdom."[6] Therefore, to understand Mormonism, one needs to clarify the essential elements of individual salvation. Robert Millet provides insight in this area

---

2. *Principles of the Gospel*, 276. Italics included in the original.

3. Robert Millet, *A Different Jesus?*, 81, 94.

4. Ibid., 95. Italics included in the original.

5. "Christ's resurrection broke the bonds of death, so that our spirit and our body will be permanently reunited" (*Principles of the Gospel*, 153).

6. *Principles of the Gospel*, 277.

as well: "We must work to our limit and then rely upon the merits, mercy, and grace of the Holy One of Israel to see us through the struggles of life and into life eternal (2 Nephi 31:19; Moroni 6:4)."[7] Salvation is accomplished by working and then by relying on God's grace to make up for our deficiencies. Elsewhere, the order seems to be reversed: after receiving the benefits of Christ, we must work toward our salvation.[8] President Spencer Kimball writes, "Eternal life hangs in the balance awaiting the works of man."[9] Quoting the *Journal of Discourses,* Millet says, Salvation:

> Requires all the atonement of Christ, the mercy of the Father, the pity of angels and the grace of the Lord Jesus Christ to be with us always, and then to do the very best we possibly can, to get rid of this sin within us, so that we may escape from this world into the celestial kingdom.[10]

Whatever the order, what is clear is that salvation in Mormonism requires a combination of grace and works. This explanation of working and relying on God's grace is consistent within Mormon scripture. 2 Nephi 25:23 says, "For we labor diligently to write, to persuade our children, and also our brethren, to believe in Christ, and to be reconciled to God; for we know that it is by grace that we are saved, after all we can do."

Frequently, Mormonism speaks in terms of Christ purchasing the ability to face judgement at which point we will be responsible for what we have done. "Each of us must stand before our Redeemer alone and account for what we have done."[11] Apostle LeGrand Richards said, "Jesus Christ redeemed all from the fall; he paid the price; he offered himself as a ransom; he atoned for Adam's

---

7. Robert Millet, *A Different Jesus?,* 69.

8. "To earn eternal life, men must obey the commandments of the Lord" (*Principles of the Gospel,* 157).

9. Spencer Kimball, *Miracle of Forgiveness,* 208.

10. Robert Millet, *A Different Jesus?,* 88, quoting the *Journal of Discourses,* 11:301.

11. *Ensign,* May 1989, 10.

sin, leaving us responsible only for our own sins."[12] "The atonement of Jesus Christ redeems all mankind from the fall of Adam and causes all to be answerable for their own manner of life."[13] At judgement, people will be held accountable for how well they kept the laws and ordinances of Mormonism. "Salvation comes only to those who accept and obey all the laws and ordinances . . ."[14] But what is included in the laws and ordinances? Mormonism classifies their ordinances in two categories: ordinances of salvation and ordinances for comfort and blessing. The necessary ordinances, or the ordinances of salvation include:

> Baptism, the sacrament, laying on of hands for the gift of the Holy Ghost, ordinations to offices in the priesthood, and the temple ordinances of washings and anointings, the endowment, and marriage for time and eternity are essential ordinances. These ordinances are sacred and require that we enter into solemn covenants.[15]

In addition, there are two further ordinances required for exaltation.

> Two special requirements for exaltation are the priesthood and celestial marriage, for to be like God means to be able to do ourselves that which our Father has done on this earth . . . These blessings are obtained through obedience to the ordinances and covenants of the house of the Lord.[16]

While Mormonism does teach that all people will experience a resurrection from the grave (general salvation), there are some sins that place people beyond the help of Christ. "Men can commit sins which it (the blood of Christ) can never remit."[17] "Joseph Smith taught that there were certain sins so grievous that man may

---

12. Richards, *A Marvelous Work and a Wonder*, 98.

13. *LDS Bible Dictionary*, 617.

14. *Principles of the Gospel*, 277.

15. Ibid., 227.

16. Ibid., 161.

17. *Journal of Discourses*, 4:59.

commit, that they will place the transgressors beyond the power of the atonement of Christ."[18] Brigham Young taught, "The blood of Christ will never wipe that out, your own blood must atone for it."[19] Those who have committed sins beyond the scope of the blood of Christ, must pay the price for those sins.

> Those who live lives of wickedness may also be heirs of salvation, that is, they too shall be redeemed from death and from hell eventually. These however, must suffer in hell the torments of the damned until they pay the price of their sinning, for the blood of Christ will not cleanse them.[20]

Observations about Salvation in Mormonism

Mormonism makes a distinction between general salvation (available to all) and individual salvation (available to a few). Grace is that which covers what is lacking after all we can do.[21] The ultimate goal of a Mormon is to achieve exaltation and become like God. While Christ died for all people, Christ's atonement serves only for general salvation and deals only with the effects of Adam's transgression and does not cover all sin. Individual salvation (exaltation) requires strict observance to the laws and ordinances. While Christ's atoning blood covers sin, there are some sins that can only be remitted through human works. The goal of Mormonism is completed when one reaches the highest heaven and becomes like God.

Questions:

1. When it comes to a biblical view of salvation and the Mormon view as contained in Mormon literature, are there differences?

2. If there are differences, are these differences significant?

---

18. *Doctrines of Salvation*, 1:138.

19. *Journal of Discourses*, 3:247.

20. *Doctrines of Salvation*, 2:133–34.

21. For an illustration of this, see Robinson, *Believing Christ*, 32, 33.

3. Without having to state which position is "right," or "wrong," are we justified in saying, at least at this one particular point, Christianity and Mormonism are not the same?

We must conclude that the elements of salvation as portrayed in the Bible are much different from those portrayed in Mormon literature. One must admit that there are significant differences.

11

Scripture

"Later-day Saints hold a view of canon that does not restrict itself to God's revelations of the past . . . Their view is broader: the canon is not closed, nor will it ever be . . . Future revelation is not only viewed as theoretically possible; it is needed and expected."[1]

—Robert Millet

The Bible's Teaching and Scripture

THE BIBLE claims that it is the living and enduring word of God (1 Peter 1:23). Although written by man, it is authored by God having been God breathed (2 Timothy 3:16). As the Word of God, it is eternal (Psalm 119:89), flawless (Proverbs 30:5), and a source of hope (Psalm 119:74). Its precepts are righteous and trustworthy (Psalms 119:42, 172), and by it man can be truly sanctified (John 17:17). As the Word of God, the Bible will stand for time and eternity (Psalm 119:89). Jesus, himself, said, "The Scriptures cannot be broken" (John 10:35).

As far as content, the Bible affirms that it contains all that is necessary for man to know about life and godliness.

All Scripture is God-breathed and is useful for teaching, rebuking, correcting and training in righteousness, so that the

---

1. Millet, *A Different Jesus?*, 10.

man of God may be thoroughly equipped for every good work.
(2 Timothy 3:16)

As the authors of Scripture wrote, they understood fully that they were writing Scripture and recognized the writings of others who wrote as well. Peter writes:

> Just as our dear brother Paul also wrote to you with the wisdom God gave him. He writes this same way in all his letters . . . His letters contain some things that are hard to understand, which ignorant and unstable people distort, as they do the other Scriptures. (2 Peter 3:15–16)

Paul commends those who heed his teaching in 1 Thessalonians, "When you received the word of God, which you heard from us, you accepted it not as the word of men, but as it actually is, the word of God" (1 Thessalonians 2:13). Not only did Paul understand that he was communicating God's word, but he understood it to be God's complete word. "I have become its servant by the commission God gave me to present to you the word of God in its fullness" (Colossians 1:25). In Galatians Paul writes, "The gospel . . . is not something that man made up. I did not receive it from any man, nor was I taught it; rather, I received it by revelation from Jesus Christ" (Galatians 1:11–12).

Perhaps the clearest testimony to the authority of Scriptures comes from the hand of Peter.

> And we have the word of the prophets made more certain, and you will do well to pay attention to it, as to a light shining in a dark place . . . Above all, you must understand that no prophecy of Scripture came about by the prophet's own interpretation. For prophecy never had its origin in the will of man, but men spoke from God as they were carried along by the Holy Spirit. (2 Peter 1:19–21)

So reliable are the words of Scripture, that the Bible warns that if a prophet ever speaks a single word that does not come true, he is not a prophet of God.

> I will put my words in his mouth, and he will tell them every-
> thing I command him. If anyone does not listen to my words
> that the prophet speaks in my name, I myself will call him to
> account. But a prophet who presumes to speak in my name
> anything I have not commanded him to say, or a prophet who
> speaks in the name of other gods, must be put to death. You
> may say to yourselves, "How can we know when a message has
> not been spoken by the Lord?" If what a prophet proclaims in
> the name of the Lord does not take place or come true, that is
> a message the Lord has not spoken. That prophet has spoken
> presumptuously. (Deuteronomy 18:18–22)

In fact, Paul warns that even if an apostle or an angel were to preach something new, the teaching cannot be allowed to change the sure and abiding word of God. "But even if we or an angel from heaven should preach a gospel other than the one we preached to you, let him be eternally condemned!" (Galatians 1:8).

As the inspired, written word, man must be bound to the Bible, guided by it, and must live by it. "Do your best to present yourself to God as one approved, a workman who does not need to be ashamed and who correctly handles the word of truth" (2 Timothy 2:15).

Observations about the Bible as Scripture

The Bible claims for itself a position of inerrancy. Inerrancy means that when all the facts are known, the Scriptures in their original copies and properly interpreted are God's Word to man, wholly true in everything they affirm, whether it has to do with doctrine or morality, or with other areas of life. The sixty-six books of the Bible contain all the truth necessary to bring an individual to sal-vation and to enable them to live godly lives and no more "truth" is needed in any previous or future generation. The Bible promises that God's Word should not be added to, or taken away from, and that it will remain forever, the abiding Word of God.

Mormon Teaching about Scripture

While Mormons consider the Bible to be one of their standard works, they do not believe it to be complete, up-to-date, necessarily correct, or unchangeable.

> Latter-day Saints feel a deep allegiance to the Bible . . . The Bible does in fact contain much that can and should guide our walk and talk; it contains the word and will of the Lord to men and women in earlier ages . . . But we do not derive authority to speak or act in the name of Deity on the basis of what God gave to his people in an earlier day.[2]

While granting that the Bible was the Word of God for an earlier audience, new revelation is needed for a new age. The Ninth Article of Faith for the LDS Church says, "We believe that He will yet reveal many great and important things pertaining to the Kingdom of God."[3] Continuing revelation is not only necessary, but is to be expected.

> The canon of scripture is not full. God has never revealed at any time that he would cease to speak forever to men . . . Modern revelation is necessary . . . We must and do believe that he continues to speak.[4]

Robert Millet writes:

> Latter-day Saints hold a view of canon that does not restrict itself to God's revelations of the past . . . the canon is not closed, nor will it ever be . . . Future revelation is not only viewed as theoretically possible; it is needed and expected.[5]

His words are in keeping with historical Mormon teaching.

> One of the great heresies of modern Christendom is the unfounded assumption that the Bible contains all of the inspired teachings now extant among men. Foreseeing that Satan

---

2. Robert Millet, *A Different Jesus?*, 78.

3. *Doctrine and Covenants*, Articles of Faith.

4. *Gospel Doctrine*, 36.

5. Robert Millet, *A Different Jesus?*, 10.

would darken the minds of men in this way, and knowing that other scripture would come forth in the last days, Nephi prophesied that unbelieving Christians would reject the new revelation with the cry: 'A Bible! A Bible! We have got a Bible, and there cannot be any more Bible.[6]

Not only does Mormonism teach that the Bible is not complete, it is not accurate.[7] Robert Millet writes:

> We do not believe in prophetic or apostolic infallibility. Latter-day Saints acknowledge that in the past men of God have been moved upon by the Holy Spirit, but we believe that prophets and apostles are men, 'subject to like passions as we are.' They are God's covenant spokesman, authorized and empowered to declare his word and lead his children, but they are not perfect.[8]

"Ignorant translators, careless transcribers, or designing and corrupt priests have committed many errors."[9] The Book of Mormon itself records:

> . . . The Bible, in its original form, "contained the plainness of the gospel of the Lord." After it had passed through the hands of a "great and abominable church, which is most abominable above all other churches," however, he saw that "many plain and precious things 'were deleted,' in consequence of which error and falsehood poured into the various churches." (1 Nephi 13, Book of Mormon)

Robert Millet writes plainly, "Latter-day Saints do not subscribe to a position of scriptural inerrancy."[10] Later he adds, "We do not believe that the hand of God has been over the preservation of the biblical materials."[11]

---

6. Bruce McConkie, *Mormon Doctrine*, 83.

7. The eighth Article of Faith for the Mormon Church states, "We believe the Bible to be the Word of God in so far as it is translated correctly."

8. Robert Millet, *A Different Jesus?*, xiv.

9. *Teachings of the Prophet Joseph Smith*, 327.

10. Robert Millet, *A Different Jesus?*, 37.

11. Robert Millet, *A Different Jesus?*, 45.

Dallin H. Oaks writes clearly and succinctly:

> What makes us different from most other Christians in the way we read and use the Bible and other scriptures is our belief in continuing revelation. *For us, the scriptures are not the ultimate source of knowledge, but what precedes the ultimate source.* The ultimate knowledge comes by revelation . . . through those we sustain as prophets, seers, and revelators.[12]

"Latter-day Saints believe the final word on prophetic interpretation rests with prophets."[13] "When prophets, who are inspired by the Holy Ghost, speak, their words take precedence over other statements on the same issue."[14] "The Kingdom of God on earth is presided over by the President of the Church, who is a prophet, seer, and revelator and who holds all of the keys for administering the work of the Church."[15]

> Next unto God and Christ, in the earth is placed one unto whom the keys of power and authority of the Holy Priesthood are conferred, and unto whom the right of presidency is given. He is God's mouthpiece to His people, in all things pertaining to the building up of Zion, and to the spiritual and temporal salvation of the people. He is God's vice-regent.[16]

One must ask then, "If the Bible is incomplete and inaccurate, and can be changed by modern prophets and revelations, what value is there in studying these scriptures?" Robert Millet answers this question for us. Please read the following two paragraphs carefully.

> Though the study of scripture may not be considered a sacramental act, Latter-day Saints believe that one essential key to the receipt of *individual* revelation—to know the mind and

---

12. Dallin H. Oaks, as quoted by Millet, *A Different Jesus?*, 16. Italics included in the original.

13. Robert Millet, *A Different Jesus?*, 51.

14. *Teachings of the Living Prophets*, 18.

15. *Principles of the Gospel*, 127.

16. Joseph F. Smith, quoted in *Achieving a Celestial Marriage*, 147.

will of God in one's life, and to come to know God—is the study of *institutional* revelation.[17]

Latter-day Saints do not hesitate to read the Bible through the lenses of the Book of Mormon, modern scripture, and the words of living apostles and prophets.[18]

Observations about Mormon Scripture

While the Bible contained God's word for a previous generation, it is not infallible or complete. Modern revelation is needed to correct and expound on past teaching. God continues to speak through his prophets today and while the current prophets remain fallible and do not bring the final word to man, they are responsible for overseeing current doctrine. The study of previous Scripture better enable God's people to receive more revelation. All previous Scripture needs to be viewed through the lense of the current apostles and prophets.

Questions:

1. When it comes to a biblical view of Scripture and the Mormon view as contained in Mormon literature, are there differences?

2. If there are differences, are these differences significant?

3. Without having to state which position is "right," or "wrong," are we justified in saying, Christianity and Mormonism are not the same?

We must conclude that the view of the Bible in regard to what constitutes Scripture and the view of the Bible as portrayed in Mormon literature are not the same. One must admit that there are significant differences.

---

17. Robert Millet, *A Different Jesus?*, 16.

18. Ibid., 60.

12

Further Differences

"From a Latter-day Saint perspective, humankind did not sud-
denly spring into existence at the time of their mortal birth. We
have always lived."[1]

—Robert Millet

THE DIFFERENCES continue between the Bible and Mormon
literature. A comprehensive study of every major doctrine
provides similar results.

Creation Is Different

The very first verse of the Bible (Genesis 1:1) begins by declaring
one of the most fundamental things we can know about God and
the world: God created the heavens and the earth. Over one hun-
dred passages of scripture in the Bible talk about God's creation, including almost every book in both the Old and New Testaments.

Mormonism, however, teaches that matter is eternal and
that God organized (or reorganized) preexistent, uncreated matter rather than creating it. Here are a few examples of Mormon
teaching about creation. "To assert that the Lord made this earth
out of nothing is preposterous and impossible. God never made
something out of nothing."[2]

---

1. Millet, *A Different Jesus?*, 18.

2. Brigham Young, *Journal of Discourses*, 14:116.

> Now the word create . . . does not mean to create out of noth-
> ing; it means to organize; the same as a man would organize
> materials and build a ship. Hence, we infer that God had ma-
> terials to organize the world out of chaos.[3]

> Under the direction of the Father, who is designated as "God
> the First, the Creator," and in company with "the noble and
> great ones," Christ created this world and all things on the face
> of it.[4]

"In addition, he became the Creator of worlds without number"
(D&C 76:24; Moses 1:33).

> In the beginning the head of the Gods called a council of the
> Gods; and they came together and concocted a plan to create
> and populate the world and people it.[5]

"The Gods organized and formed the heavens and earth. And they
[the Gods] said: Let there be light; and there was light. And they
[the Gods] comprehended the light. And the Gods called the light
day" (Pearl of Great Price, Book of Abraham, 4:1–5).

Heaven Is Different

In Mormonism, heaven is divided in three separate and distinct
kingdoms: the celestial kingdom, the terrestrial kingdom and the
telestial kingdom. "The level of glory we receive in the resurrection will depend upon the level of law that we have obeyed during
this life."[6]

> The celestial is the dwelling place of God. The highest of
> its three degrees will be inherited only by those who have
> received exaltation [become Gods]. In addition to faith in
> Christ, repentance, baptism, the laying on of hands for the gift
> of the Holy Ghost, and obedience to all the Lord's commands,

---

3. *Teachings of the Prophet Joseph Smith*, 350–51.

4. Pearl of Great Price, *Book of Abraham*, 3:22–24; 4:1.

5. *Journal of Discourses*, 6:5.

6. *Principles of the Gospel*, 223.

they must have been sealed in the everlasting covenant of celestial marriage and must have kept the conditions of that covenant.[7]

The terrestrial kingdom is composed of those,

Who receive of the presence of the Son, but not the fullness of the Father. Four major groups of people who will inherit this glory: Accountable persons who die without hearing the celestial law and who do not accept it. Those who reject the gospel in this life, but reverse their course in the spirit world. The honorable men of the earth who were blinded. Members of the Church of Jesus Christ who were not valiant.[8]

The telestial kingdom is that degree of glory which apparently will be inherited by a large number of adult people who live upon the earth . . . These are they who receive not of his fullness in the eternal world, but of the Holy Spirit.[9]

Hell Is Different

Mormon hell is not eternal and is reserved only for those "known as the sons of perdition, who have received the Holy Spirit and then denied it, who are in open, willful rebellion against the truth."[10]

Baptism Is Different

"Baptism for the dead [proxy baptism] is the means whereby all God's worthy children of all ages can become heirs of salvation. It is for those of apostate darkness where the gospel light does not shine."[11]

---

7. Ibid., 202.

8. Ibid., 204.

9. Ibid., 205.

10. Ibid.

11. McConkie, *Mormon Doctrine*, 73.

Marriage Is Different

"Celestial marriage binds couples together for time and eternity and is the gate to an exaltation in the highest heaven within the celestial world. It is the most important thing any member of the Church of Jesus Christ of Latter-day Saints ever does."[12]

Communion Is Different

Orson Pratt writes, "All other churches are entirely destitute of all authority from God; and any person who receives Baptism or the Lord's supper from their hands will highly offend God, for he looks upon them as the most corrupt of all people."[13] Also, water is used in place of grape juice or wine.[14] According to the *Encyclopedia of Mormonism*, "All members of the Church, including unbaptized children, are encouraged to partake of the bread and water as emblems in remembrance of the body and blood of Jesus Christ."[15]

A close examination of major doctrines shows that Mormonism and evangelical Christianity disagree on major doctrinal issues—not small disagreements, but often views completely antithetical. This being true, how can one consider Christianity and Mormonism to be "the same?"

---

12. Ibid., 118.

13. Pratt, *The Seer*, 255.

14. McConkie, *Mormon Doctrine*, 661.

15. See page 299.

Conclusion

Ministering (Living) in a Mormon Context

RECENTLY, AFTER presenting a workshop on the differences between Mormonism and Evangelical Christianity, an LDS woman (along with her two daughters) came up to me, weeping. Struggling to find words she said, "I've known in my heart for some time that something was not right [with what I believed], but I didn't know any better. I've talked to friends who belong to a Christian church, and have even discussed my misgivings briefly with a Christian minister, but I didn't see any differences. Honestly, until tonight, I'm not sure I knew there *were* differences." Then she asked me this heart wrenching question: "Why has no one told me this before?"

This question is worth further exploration. Why hasn't anyone effectively explained the differences? While some may be content to make excuses or dismiss this as an anomaly, my experience ministering in southern Idaho has convinced me that this woman is not alone in her confusion. Many Mormons do not know what the LDS church teaches and, therefore, do not know what they believe. Unfortunately, this malady is equally true within the walls of Christian churches—many Christians are ignorant of their own beliefs. Few people from either camp are able to clearly articulate their faith, and fewer still can compare what they believe with their religious neighbor.

To complicate matters, there are others who are convinced that perceived differences are merely misunderstandings; or they have succumbed to recent media ploys and believe that Mormonism has actually moved toward Evangelical Christianity.

At this point, I must ask my own question: "How can someone become part of a church without knowing what that particular church believes?" The answer reveals a sad fact. Rather than choosing a church based on particular doctrinal beliefs, people often make choices based on family, friends, feelings, and festivities. Some people belong to a certain church because of their family history—they grew up in that church. Other people are attracted to a particular church by friends or neighbors who reached out to them. Others still are drawn in by community programs. While no one should question the benefits and attractive nature of fellowship and activities, all who are earnestly seeking the truth should readily admit that proper doctrine is paramount. This being the case, something must be done to educate people in what they believe and why.

Something Must Be Done

In light of the recent attempts of the LDS Church to appear within the realms of mainstream Christianity, this issue is pressing—Christian churches must take action! Both the Church and the individual Christian must respond to the LDS movement. Two things must happen if the church is to successfully confront the presence of Mormonism. First, the church must respond by teaching, equipping, and training people within its congregation in regards to proper doctrine. Second, the individual Christian must be willing to learn and take a stand for truth. Paul gives this instruction: "Do your best to present yourself to God as one approved, a workman who does not need to be ashamed and who correctly handles the word of truth" (2 Timothy 2:15).

In this chapter, will address both of these needed responses. In addition, at the end of this chapter, I have included several appendices that might help one to minister in a Mormon context. My prayer is that this material will help each of us more effectively handle the truth of God's word.

How Must the Christian Church Respond to Mormonism?

The church must begin by recognizing its failures. The church has failed to teach biblical doctrine to its people. The best way to spot a counterfeit bill is to study the real thing. Educating people toward biblical literacy must become a priority. Mormonism often preys on the ignorance and half-learned lessons of the immature Christian and non-Christian. Mormonism proclaims a "new truth" or a "restored truth" to people who have too little of the "old truth." The Christian church must take preventive measures to keep its people from leaving the fold. The church must lead "milk-drinking" Christians to become "meat-eaters" (Hebrews 5:14). How can the church accomplish this?[1]

The Church Must Alter Its Preaching

1. The church can no longer afford to preach shallow sermons, but must provide a steady diet of doctrinal, expository sermons on the essentials of Christianity.[2] Sermons on the nature of God, the deity of Christ, the tri-unity of God, and the substitutionary atonement of Christ's sacrifice are essential.

2. The church must preach biblical absolutes. There is such a thing as absolute truth and it is essential that the church make this a platform of its teaching. Situational ethics are not and must not become the basis for right and wrong. Truth is not relative, but by its very nature is exclusive.

3. The church must emphasize the Bible as the unchangeable word of God.

---

1. The following material in this chapter reflects information first presented to me by Boise Bible College professor, Dale Cornett in a class he taught on Mormonism. I have altered, adapted, and expanded some of that material.

2. For an excellent treatment of doctrinal preaching, see: Jeff A. Spry, *The Preparation and Delivery of Expository Doctrinal Sermons*, (D.Min thesis project, Gordon-Conwell Theological Seminary, 2007).

The Church Must Intensify Its Teaching

1. Christianity is a taught religion, and it is often not taught well. The church must give clear and precise definitions of words and key principles.

2. The church must provide doctrinal and exegetical teaching from prepared teachers.

3. The church must provide courses on Mormonism (and other religious systems) to educate its members.

4. The church must train its people to question, challenge, and be loyal to the Bible.

5. The church must develop quality shepherding systems and strong youth programs.

6. The church must emphasize Bible-college and seminary training for church leaders.

7. The church must build strong libraries within its walls.

8. The church must unite together with other churches to take a stand against false doctrine.

The Church Must Meet the Spiritual and Emotional Needs of Its Members

1. Churches have not provided the love, the fellowship, the caring, the sharing, the personal interest, or the family atmosphere that they should promote. Meanwhile, Mormonism has excelled in these areas. Lonely, frustrated Christians are ripe for Mormonism.

2. Churches must provide vibrant worship. Worship services are too often dead and boring, with little "worship" really going on.

3. The church must not be afraid to require genuine commitment and sacrifice. Mormonism is not afraid to require com-

mitment from its members, why should the church require any less?

4. The church must call on Mormons like they call on others. To accomplish this, it must train its callers as effectively as they train theirs.

5. Classes on evangelism must be taught.

6. Calling programs must be launched utilizing the people in the pew.

How Must the Individual Christian Respond to the Cults?

You Must Prepare Yourself for Hard Work

1. You must prepare your heart.

2. You must spend time in prayer, making sure that your personal attitudes stay in check and your motivations remain pure. You need to spend time in earnest and intimate prayer with God daily.

3. You must keep positive attitudes, always remembering to love others unconditionally.

4. You must not argue.

5. You must prepare your mind.

6. You must not only know biblical doctrine, you must familiarize yourself with Mormon teaching. Knowing Mormon documents as well as Mormon doctrines is fundamental.

7. You must be able to respond biblically. You should make a list of Scriptures which speak directly to various teaching and include it in your Bible. Better yet, you should memorize them.

8. You must prepare for action.

9. You must look for opportunities and be ready and willing to speak when those opportunities arise. When an opportunity

presents itself, it is helpful to take a deep breath, say a quick prayer, and speak with as much boldness as possible, trusting the Holy Spirit to guide your thoughts.

You Must Present the Gospel Truth to Mormons

1. Pray with them and for them.

2. Establish common ground.

3. Ask specifically what they believe about God. (If they say they believe like you, ask them to define terms. Write down their definitions).

4. Use their version of Scripture—The King James Version (KJV). Be committed to the Bible as the unassailable witness of truth. Mormons will probably have some residual mistrust of the Bible.

5. Stick to the key issues. At first, stick to ONE subject—the Mormon Doctrine of God. Ask for one verse of Scripture from the Book of Mormon that supports their position about God. They cannot give it. Don't get sidetracked. Mormons are often taught to change the subject rather than answering difficult questions. Try to keep them on topic.

6. Be prepared and be specific. Learn how to ask questions that get to core issues. If you speak in general terms, clear differences will be left unexposed.

7. Challenge them to study the Bible and think for themselves. Mormons are taught not to question the authority of the LDS church. If you can get them to start reading and studying the Bible on their own, you will have opened the door for their exit from Mormonism.

8. Give a personal testimony. This is a key ingredient within the LDS faith and your testimony will be highly effective when speaking with Mormons. Speak with them about your conver-

sion, specifically that you are a sinner saved by grace and not works. Tell about your relationship with Jesus Christ and what he has done for you. Talk about your freedom in Christ.

9. Stress Christ, not some church. Make sure you convert the heart of a person to Jesus, not just to yourself or to your church.

10. If unable to win them, then in love, warn them of the judgement of God on all perversions of His gospel. Challenge them to carefully study what they believe compared to what their Bible says.

11. Thank them for sharing with you and invite them back. Let them know that you are willing to talk again if they have questions in the future.

12. You must persevere. Mormons can be won, but only by consistency, commitment, and hard work. Take the initiative, and keep at it. For example, when speaking to a Mormon missionary who has come to your door, say, "You may come in IF I may ask you some questions about your church."

13. Be ready to invest your life in them. Few Mormons are won quickly or easily. Most Mormons, if they leave their church, leave behind their whole safety net and social structure. We must realize that Mormonism is not just a belief system, but a culture. They need somewhere to turn and someone to turn to.

14. Pray that you can be used by God and that he will direct your conversations. Ultimately, you must remember that it is not your words or arguments that will affect change, but God's word. "For the word of God is living and active. Sharper than any double-edged sword, it penetrates even to dividing soul and spirit, joints and marrow; it judges the thoughts and attitudes of the heart" (Hebrews 4:12).

APPENDIX A

Understanding the Strategies of Mormon Missionaries

IN ORDER to effectively preach in a Mormon context, it is helpful to know the approach Mormon missionaries will use when proselytizing members of your community. After missionaries make an initial contact (either by canvassing neighborhoods or by delivering a Bible or a requested Book of Mormon), the next step is to get a person to view various tapes or videos. Current titles include "The Heavenly Father's Plan" and "On the Way Home." Following these videos, there are six lessons missionaries will attempt to teach. Here is an outline of the standard curriculum commonly used by Mormon missionaries.

Lesson One—The Plan of Our Heavenly Father

1. God, the Father, has a plan for our happiness. It is called the plan of salvation.

2. Jesus Christ has a central mission in the plan.

3. God reveals the truth about his plan through prophets.

4. The prophet, Joseph Smith, is a modern witness of Jesus Christ. Through him, God has restored knowledge about the divine plan.

5. The Book of Mormon is another testament of Jesus Christ that clearly explains the divine plan.

6. Through the Holy Ghost each person can know that this message is true.[1]

Lesson Two—The Gospel of Jesus Christ

1. Through the resurrection, we will be saved from physical death.

2. Through obedience to the principles and ordinances of the gospel of Jesus Christ, we can also be saved from sin.

3. In order to make the atonement effective in our lives, we must have faith in Christ.

4. We must repent of our sins.

5. We must be baptized by immersion to enter into a covenant with God.

6. We must receive the gift of the Holy Ghost to be spiritually reborn.

7. We must strive to obey all the commandments of God.[2]

Lesson Three—The Restoration

1. Divine truth does not come from human sources. It comes from God, who revealed the truth through his apostles and prophets.

2. Because of the apostasy, the gift of revelation was lost for centuries.

3. God has again revealed the truth in our day through apostles and prophets of his restored church.

4. Through Joseph Smith, God restored the priesthood and reestablished the church of Jesus Christ.

---

1. *Uniform System for Teaching the Gospel*, 1-1.

2. Ibid., 2-1.

5. We must come unto Christ by joining his church.

6. The members of the church receive great blessings by attending church meetings and partaking of the sacrament.[3]

Lesson Four—Eternal Progression

1. Before this mortal life, we lived with our Father in heaven.

2. The purpose of this mortal life is for us to prepare to become more like our Heavenly Father and return to him.

3. When we die, our spirits go to the spirit world.

4. The gospel is taught to the spirits in the spirit world, and the necessary ordinances are performed for them in temples.

5. The family can be an eternal unit.

6. The law of chastity teaches us how to govern the sacred power of procreation.

7. The word of wisdom is a divine law of health.[4]

Lesson Five—Living a Christ-like Life

1. We should love God and our fellow men.

2. Sacrifice brings blessings.

3. Fasting and fast offerings bring us spiritual blessings.

4. The law of tithing helps us develop selflessness.[5]

Lesson Six—Membership in the Kingdom

1. Jesus Christ is our Creator, Redeemer, Savior, and Judge.

---

3. Ibid., 3-1.
4. Ibid., 4-1.
5. Ibid., 5-1.

2. Exaltation comes through Christ, and his church helps us progress toward perfection.

3. The church and its members have a responsibility for perfecting the saints.

4. The church and its members have a responsibility for proclaiming the gospel.

5. The church and its members have a responsibility for redeeming the dead.

6. We can follow the straight and narrow path to perfection.[6]

Prospective converts are also frequently introduced to *Gospel Principles* which gives an overview of church doctrine.

---

6. Ibid., 6-1.

APPENDIX B

Understanding Mormon Vocabulary

A MAJOR DIFFICULTY in witnessing to Mormons is that they have a different vocabulary. Not only have they coined numerous words that are unique to Mormonism, but they frequently give unique definitions to biblical words. The following definitions will help you decipher what Mormonism teaches. It is important that you remember that the following definitions are not biblical or Christian definitions, but LDS definitions.

Aaronic Priesthood. Known as the lesser priesthood. It serves as the entry point into the priesthood for boys twelve and older and adult male converts. It includes deacons, teachers, priests, and bishops.

Adam. The first man; the father of the human race. Before his earthly life, he was known as Michael, the Archangel, and the Ancient of Days. He led the righteous in the war in heaven and helped create the earth. Mormons believe he was the Heavenly Father's finest spirit child. He was sent to earth to make man mortal, which he accomplished through the fall. Mormons consider this fall good.

Administer the Sacrament. To bless communion before it is taken.

Agency. The ability to choose right and wrong which began during man's pre-existence.

Age of Accountability. The age at which a person becomes responsible for his or her actions and may be baptized; in most cases, eight years old.

Ancient of Days. See Adam.

Angels. Not creatures of God distinct from humans as the Bible teaches. Most often defined as a resurrected or translated body.

Anoint. To place a few drops of oil on the head, usually as part of a priesthood blessing.

Apostasy. Turning away from or leaving the teachings of the LDS church. The great apostasy happened after the apostles and remained until Joseph Smith restored the church. During the Apostasy, the truth of the gospel vanished from the face of the earth.

Apostle. A person called and appointed to be a special witness for Christ. An office in the Melchizedek Priesthood.

Articles of Faith. Thirteen brief statements written by the prophet Joseph Smith describing the basic teachings and ordinances of the church. They do not mention any of the distinctive Mormon doctrines.

Atonement. The suffering and death of Jesus in the Garden of Gethsemane through which resurrection is provided to all. It speaks of Jesus paying the price for sins, but this price must be paid back by obeying the fullness of gospel laws. While atonement grants the right to be resurrected, it does not determine where eternity will be spent.

Authority. See Priesthood.

Baptism. By immersion either at the age of eight or when converted to the church. Must be performed by a holder of the priesthood.

Baptism for the Dead. One of the three main missions of the LDS church. Used to redeem the dead by being baptized for them. Mormons believe that spirits who accept Mormonism in the spirit world cannot progress until they are baptized. These baptisms can only be performed at the temple.

Bear a Testimony. A popular expression for giving a testimony about the truth of Mormonism.

Benson, Ezra Taft (1899–1994). Became Mormonism's thirteenth President in 1985.

Bible. One of four books Mormons consider Scripture. Not trustworthy in the eyes of most Mormons because is has been corrupted. It is the word of God only "as far as it is translated correctly." They believe many precious parts have been lost from it. They consider it the least reliable of their Scriptures. The Mormon Church has gone to great lengths to discredit the authority of the Bible.

Bishop. The head of the local ward (congregation). He also presides over the Aaronic Priesthood. One of the major criteria for becoming a bishop is success in the business or professional world. They usually have no formal theological training. Most serve five years.

Book of Abraham. A section of the Pearl of Great Price. Talks about the gods creating the world and about Kolob, the star closest to God's throne. Joseph Smith claimed to have translated it from Egyptian papyri.

Book of Commandments. A collection of Joseph Smith's early revelations, printed in 1833. These were added to other revelations and renamed the Doctrine and Covenants in 1835. See Doctrine and Covenants.

Book of Mormon. One of the standard works of the LDS Church. It is an account of God's dealings with the people of the American continents from about 2,200 years before the birth of Jesus Christ to 421 years after his death. It was supposedly translated from gold plates by Joseph Smith and is said to contain the fulness of the gospel. The introduction to the Book of Mormon reads, "I told the brethren that the Book of Mormon was the most correct of any book on earth, and the keystone of our religion, and a man would get nearer to God by abiding by its precepts, than by any other book."

Book of Moses. A section of the Pearl of Great Price. Contains teachings on the plurality of gods, Adam's "good" fall, and Satan's rebellion.

Branch. A developing ward. Too small to qualify as a ward.

Burning in the Bosom. A feeling of peace and assurance that is used to confirm the truthfulness of the Book of Mormon or an individual's action.

Called. To be assigned a duty or position in the church.

Celestial Kingdom. The highest of three kingdoms of LDS heaven. At this level, exaltation is possible. The Celestial Kingdom is the only place where Heavenly Father resides and governs. Only those who have kept the whole Mormon law will one day be exalted to this level.

Celestial Marriage. Being married in a Mormon Temple for time and eternity.

Church News. A weekly periodical reporting LDS Church news and events.

Church of the Firstborn. The highest of three levels in the celestial kingdom. Only Mormons who keep all the commandments of God will enter this heaven and become Gods in eternity.

Clerk. The member in the ward who keeps track of church attendance and other data. During meetings he sits up front taking attendance and recording statistics.

Comprehensive History of the Church. A six-volume history of the Mormon Church compiled by Mormon historian Brigham H. Roberts.

Conference. See General Conference.

Council in Heaven. The meeting in heaven in which Heavenly Father announced the plan of salvation and chose Jesus Christ as our redeemer.

Counselors. Every organization of the church, at every level of the church, is run by a presidency that consists of a president and two counselors.

Create. To organize eternal matter, in contrast to the biblical description of creating out of nothing.

Creation. Guided by the Father and organized by Jesus Christ. Many preexistent spirit children also participated in the creation of this world.

Cross. Mormons are repulsed by symbols of Christ's cross. They do not exhibit crosses in their meeting houses or homes. They usually will not wear them as jewelry. They view it as a symbol of death and believe Christ's sacrifice occurred at Gethsemene not on the cross.

Cumorah. The hill in western New York where the gold plates containing the Book of Mormon were supposedly hidden and subsequently found by Joseph Smith.

Deacon. Twelve to fourteen-year-old boys who are chosen to tasks in the church.

Demons. Spirit children who joined Satan in his rebellion. They were deprived of any chance of continuing progression to godhood.

Deseret. The Book of Mormon name for honeybee (Ether 2:3). Used in names of LDS businesses because it implies industry.

Devil. A spirit son of God who rebelled against the Father and tried to destroy the free will of man.

Doctrine and Covenants. One of the standard works of the LDS Church, containing revelations given to Joseph Smith and other Latter-day presidents of the Church.

Doctrines of Salvation. A three-volume set of doctrinal writings authored by tenth LDS President Joseph Fielding Smith. Compiled in 1954.

Documentary History of the Church. Also known as the *History of the Church* or *DHC*. A seven-volume set expounding on the history of the Mormon Church.

Elder. The lowest ordained office of the Melchizedek priesthood. This gives Mormons the authority to teach, expound, exhort, baptize, and watch over the church. Also known as a standing home minister.

Elohim. The Hebrew word for God. Mormons identify it exclusively with Heavenly Father. Jesus was Jehovah (translated Lord in English), although the Bible often uses both names in reference to the same person.

Endowment. A gift of power given through ordinances in the temple to worthy members of the Church. Includes being ceremonially washed, receiving a new name, sacred garments and learning various handshakes that are essential for exaltation.

Ensign. A monthly magazine published by the LDS Church covering Mormon news, events, and doctrinal and policy issues.

Eternal Families. The promise that "families are forever" for those who are worthy and have had their families sealed to them in Mormon Temples.

Eternal Increase. The ability to procreate throughout eternity.

Eternal Life. Another name for godhood and synonymous with exaltation; living externally as God. Officially distinct from immortality. It does not describe living with God, but living as God.

Eternal Marriage. See Celestial Marriage.

Eternal Progression. The concept that a person can progress through three estates (premortal, mortal, post-mortal), eventually obtaining godhood.

Eternal Punishment. Not punishment forever, but rather punishment from God whose name is eternal (See Doctrine and Covenants 19:10–12).

Exaltation. The highest state of happiness and glory in the Celestial Kingdom. Godhood.

Excommunication. A process by which an LDS membership is terminated.

Exemplar. A popular LDS title for Jesus. It reveals the Mormon's belief that Jesus saved them by being an example, not by becoming their substitute.

Fall. Gave mankind the ability to have children and thus is good.

Family Home Evening. Every Monday, families are to spend time together studying and playing. No church activities are scheduled for Monday night.

Fast Offering. Contribution to the Church of the money or commodities saved by fasting for two consecutive meals.

First Estate. See pre-mortal existence.

First Presidency. The President of the Church and his two counselors.

First Vision. The vision Joseph Smith supposedly received in 1820 when he was told not to join any church since they were all corrupt.

Forgiveness. Granted when all the commandments of the Lord are kept. "Your Heavenly Father has promised forgiveness upon total repentance and meeting all the requirements, but that forgiveness is not granted merely for the asking. There must be works—many works . . . It depends upon you whether or not you are forgiven, and when. It could be weeks, it could be years, it could be centuries before that happy day when you have the positive assurance that the Lord has forgiven you" (*Miracle of Forgiveness*, Spencer W. Kimball, 324).

Fulness of the Gospel. All the ordinances and laws of the LDS gospel.

Garden of Eden. One located in the central part of the United States near Jackson County, Missouri.

Genealogy. Researching family history for the purpose of performing temple work on behalf of the dead.

General Authority. The title for a church leader whose authority is not limited to one geographical area but is general. Consists of the First Presidency of the Church, the Quorum of the Twelve Apostles, the First and Second Quorums of Seventy, and the Presiding Bishopric.

General Conference. Held in Salt Lake City every April and October. General Authorities and other church leaders speak on current issues and Mormon teaching.

Gentiles. Non-Mormons.

God. The Father of Jesus Christ in the flesh and of the spirits of all humankind. God is an exalted man with flesh and bone.

Godhead. Three separate Gods: Father, Son, Holy Spirit. These three are one in purpose and plan, but not literally one God, one substance.

Golden Contact. A person who knows little or nothing about Mormonism, but is eager to learn.

Gospel. The combination of the atonement of Christ, baptism, laying on of hands to receive the Holy Spirit, temple endowments, temple marriage, love and worshiping God, faith in Jesus, chastity, repentance, tithing, honesty, truthfulness, obeying the Word of Wisdom, baptism for the dead, keeping the Sabbath day, attending church meetings, godly family life, daily family prayers, honoring parents, obeying the Mormon prophets, charity, and keeping all the Lord's commandments until the end of your life.

Grace. Not unconditional or undeserved, but enhanced by the good works of man. It is the power God gives people to save themselves, which he grants only after they have done everything they can do.

Grant, Heber J. (1865–1945). Became Mormonism's seventh President in 1918.

Heaven. Consists of three kingdoms: Celestial, Terrestrial, Telestial.

Hell. Not a place of eternal punishment, but the temporary state of suffering wicked spirits. After their resurrection, a great majority of people will pass from Hell into the Telestial Kingdom.

High Council. Twelve men on the stake level who assist the stake presidency.

Holy Ghost. The third member of the Godhead; a personage of spirit. The Holy Ghost is a spirit person who can only be in one place at a time but can influence the world and is the revealer and testifier of truth.

Holy Spirit. Heavenly Father's spirit and extended power—different from the Holy Ghost.

Home Teachers. Men who are given the responsibility of visiting the home of each member once a month. Their job is to encourage members to grow spiritually and perform their church duties.

Hunter, Howard (1907–1995). Became Mormonism's fourteenth President in 1994.

Inspired Version. Another name for Joseph Smith's translation of the Bible. LDS books contain excerpts of it in footnotes.

Intelligences. The part of mankind that Mormons say is eternal.

Investigator. A person talking the Mormon missionary lessons.

Jaredites. According to the Book of Mormon, they were people whose language was preserved by faith at the time of the Tower of Babel. They subsequently came to America.

Jehovah. See Jesus Christ.

Jesus Christ. The firstborn son of God. Jesus is Heavenly Father's eldest spirit child. He came to earth in spirit as Jehovah in the Old Testament. In this state he organized earth. He came to earth in body by being born to the virgin Mary. Jesus' death secured immortality (life after death) for all people and also secured the opportunity for spiritual progression by the forgiveness of sins. Each person's place in immortality remains up to the individuals and what they do during their mortal existence.

Journal of Discourses. A twenty-six-volume set of books containing sermons from various Mormon leaders until 1886.

Kimball, Spencer W. (1895–1985). Became Mormonism's twelfth President in 1973.

King Follet Sermon. The funeral sermon Joseph Smith preached in 1844 for a man named King Follett. Many Mormons consider this the greatest sermon ever preached. In it Smith outlined his thoughts on the nature of God and how man can become a god.

Kingdom of God. See Celestial Kingdom.

Kolob. The star nearest the throne of God. This is where humans live until they take human form here on earth.

Lamanites. According to the Book of Mormon, these Jews became the ancestors of the American Indians.

Lee, Harold B. (1899–1973). Became Mormonism's eleventh President in 1972.

Lehi. A righteous man who fled Jerusalem before its destruction in 600 B.C. and came to America.

Line of Authority. Every priesthood holder should be able to trace his "line of authority" back to Jesus Christ. He should know who ordained him and who ordained the person who ordained him, etc.

Lucifer. See Devil.

McKay, David O. (1873–1970). Became Mormonism's ninth President in 1951.

Mankind. The spirit children of God (Elohim) and his heavenly wife. Because mankind is the literal offspring of God, they have the potential to become gods.

Marriage. Marriages performed in the temples are for the present life and future life. The highest level of the Celestial Kingdom is only for those who have been so sealed.

Melchizedek Priesthood. The higher priesthood that worthy young men enter at the age eighteen or nineteen. Mormons believe Peter, James, and John bestowed it on Joseph Smith and Oliver Cowdery in 1829. The offices of the Melchizedek priesthood are elder, seventy, high priest, and patriarch.

Michael, the Archangel. See Adam.

Mission. A voluntary commitment to commit time and service to the Mormon missionary program. Length of service lasts eighteen months for females and two years for males.

Missionary Lessons. Known as "Uniform System for Teaching the Gospel." A series of six lessons given to investigators, which helps to explain Mormon doctrines. (See appendix "A" for outline of lessons).

Moroni. According to the Book of Mormon, he is the son of Mormon. Buried the gold plates containing the record of the Nephite people and later revealed their location to Joseph Smith.

Nauvoo. Originally known as Commerce, Illinois. This city became the headquarters of the Mormon Church until Joseph Smith's death in 1844. Literally means, "beautiful place."

Nephites. According to the Book of Mormon, these were decedents of the Jews who came to America. The Nephites became corrupt and were destroyed by the Lamanites. Much of the Book of Mormon is a description of the wars between these two groups.

Ordinances. Rites administered by the priesthood.

Outer Darkness. The place which Satan, unrighteous spirits, and extreme cases of apostasy are sent following judgment.

Pearl of Great Price. One of the standard works of the Church. Contains a collection of five brief items: the Book of Moses, the Book of Abraham, Joseph Smith—Matthew, Joseph Smith—History, and the Articles of Faith. Because of its brevity, it is usually included along with other standard works.

Plurality of Gods. Mormons prefer this term to polytheism. They claim they are not polytheists because they worship only one God.

Plural Marriage. The practice of being married to two or more women at the same time. The mainstream Mormon Church does not condone polygamy. Any splinter groups still involved in this practice are condemned by the LDS Church.

Prexistence of Spirits. The doctrine that all mankind, prior to an earthy existence, were spirit children of heavenly parents. See premortal existence.

Premortal Existence. The period between the birth of spirit children of Heavenly Father and their birth into mortal life. Called the first estate.

Priesthood. Men in the LDS Church who hold either the Aaronic or Melchizedek priesthood have authority from God. Christianity lost that authority after the death of the Lord's Apostles and has been in a state of total apostasy since then. Reviving the office of priest is one of the restoration principles.

Quad. The Bible, Book of Mormon, Doctrine and Covenants, and Pearl of Great Price bound together as one book.

Prophet. The President of the Church and the twelve apostles.

Reorganized Church of Jesus Christ of Latter-day Saints. Known as RLDS. Splinter group of the LDS movement. Headquartered in

Independence, Missouri. This group historically has been led by direct descendants of Joseph Smith, rather than the Quorum of the Twelve. The RLDS are less controversial than their LDS counterparts and do not like being called Mormons.

Restoration. The period of history ushered in by Joseph Smith. Mormons believe that after the apostles died, the true church left the earth (the great apostasy) until it was restored by Joseph Smith.

RM. Short for Returned Missionary.

Salvation. (1) The equivalent to resurrection. When Mormons say they are saved by Jesus alone, they mean that they don't have anything to do with the resurrection. Christ's death brought release from the grave and gives immortality universally. (2) Used of exaltation.

Satan. See Devil.

Sealings. An ordinance that binds a man and wife as well as their children into a family unit that will be preserved throughout eternity.

Seer. The President of the Church is often referred to as Prophet, Revelator, or Seer.

Seminary. Not a theological school, but the daily set of instructions on Mormonism offered to junior high or high school students.

Smith, George Albert (1870–1951). Became Mormonism's eighth President in 1945.

Smith, Jr., Joseph (1805–1844). Founder and first President.

Smith, Joseph F. (1838–1919). A nephew of Joseph Smith who became Mormonism's sixth President in 1901.

Smith, Joseph Fielding (1876–1972). A son of Joseph F. Smith who became Mormonism's tenth President in 1970.

Snow, Lorenzo (1814–1901). Became Mormonism's fifth President in 1898.

Sons of Perdition. The spirit hosts of heaven who followed Lucifer. Also those who gain knowledge of the Savior and then turn from him.

Spirit Prison. The place where all non-LDS people go immediately following death.

Stake. A geographical group of wards.

Standard Works. The volumes of Scripture officially accepted by the LDS Church: King James Bible, Book of Mormon, Doctrine and Covenants, and Pearl of Great Price.

Taylor, John (1808–1887). Became Mormonism's third President in 1877.

Telestial Kingdom. The lowest kingdom of heaven. It is not visited by Heavenly Father or Jesus, but only by the Holy Ghost. This will be the final destination of carnal and wicked people.

Temple Recommend. A small card that allows temple-worthy Mormons to enter the temple. To be worthy they must keep the Word of Wisdom, tithe, be morally upright, and be supportive of church leaders. This is determined in regularly scheduled interviews.

Terrestrial Kingdom. The middle kingdom of heaven. It is for those who have not heard the restored gospel as taught by the LDS, who have been good and honorable but blinded. Jesus will visit the Terrestrial Kingdom, but Heavenly Father will not.

Triple Combination. The Book of Mormon, Doctrine and Covenants, and Pearl of Great Price bound together as one book.

Vicarious Work. An expression describing temple work for the dead. Most frequently used to describe being baptized for the dead.

Virgin Birth. The Mormon doctrine of a Godhead with three separate Gods forces them to reject the Holy Ghost as the agency through which Christ' immaculate conception occurred. If Christ was conceived by the Holy Ghost, he could not be called the Son of the Father (Elohim). Instead, they teach that God the Father had a physical relationship with Mary and she conceived in the same natural way that all conceive on this earth. This doctrine destroys the biblical truth of the virgin birth (See *Family Home Evening Manual*, 1972, p. 125 or *Mormon Doctrine*, McConkie, p. 547).

Ward. The smallest unit of the LDS Church, equivalent to a local congregation. Usually more than one ward meets in the same meeting house. Wards vary in size. When a ward reaches eight-hundred members, it is divided. Wards are set up on a geographical basis and church members do not have a choice of what ward they attend.

Woodruff, Wilford (1807–1898). Became Mormonism's fourth President in 1889.

Word of Wisdom. A revelation concerning health practices given to Joseph Smith in 1833 in section 89 of the Doctrine and Covenants. It is a list of substances to indulge in or abstain from. Mormons must abstain from wine, strong drink, tobacco, etc.

Young, Brigham (1801–1877). Became Mormonism's second President in 1847.

Zion. A commonly used LDS term with a variety of meanings. Zion is where God dwells. It can refer to: (1) the Church of Jesus Christ of Latter-day Saints; (2) Utah, (3) Independence, Missouri, or (4) a condition of the heart.

APPENDIX C

Quick Reference Guide

God

Biblical Passages about God

Deuteronomy 6:4; 4:35; Isaiah 43:10; 45:5; 44:6–8; Psalm 90:2; Malachi 3:6; James 1:17; John 4:24; I Timothy 6:16; 1 Timothy 1:17.

God in Mormonism:

"Let me tell you how God came to be a God, he was once a man like us" (Joseph Smith, "The King Follett Sermon," JD 6:3).

"As Man is, God once was. As God is, man may become" (Lorenzo Snow couplet, fifth President of the church, 1898–1901).

"How has there been a God from all eternity? The answer is that there has been and there now exists an endless line of Divine Intelligences—Deities, stretching back into the eternities, that had no beginning and will have no end. Their existence runs parallel with endless duration, and their dominions are as limitless as boundless space" (B. H. Roberts, General Council).

"God the Father has a glorified, exalted body; the Father has a body of flesh and bones as tangible as man's" (D&C 130:22).

"In the Image of his own body, He created them" (Book of Moses, 2:27).

Jesus

Biblical Passages about Jesus

John 1:1, 14; John 3:16; Matthew 1:23; Isaiah 9:6; Colossians 1:16–17; Titus 2:13–14.

Jesus in Mormonism

"He is the first spirit child of Elohim, of which there are countless others" (*Principles of the Gospel*, 201).

"All men (Christ included) were born as the sons of God in the spirit, one man (Christ only) was born as the Son of God in the mortal world . . . God was his Father; Mary was his mother . . . He is the Son of God in the same literal, full, and complete sense in which he is the Son of Mary. There is nothing symbolic or figurative about it" (Bruce McConkie, *A New Witness*, 67).

"How is he the Eternal One? It might be said that he is eternal, as all men are, meaning that spirit element—the intelligence which was organized into intelligences—has always existed and is therefore eternal" (Bruce McConkie, *The Promised Messiah*, 165).

"Jesus of Nazareth is literally the Son of God . . . He is not the Son of the Father in some mystical, metaphorical sense" (Robert Millet, *A Different Jesus*, 20).

The Holy Spirit

The Bible and the Holy Spirit

1 Corinthians 2:10–11; Ephesians 4:30; Romans 15:30; 1 Corinthians 12:11; Romans 8:27; Psalms 139:7–10; Luke 1:35–37; Isaiah 40:13; Hebrews 9:14. (The same Greek word "pneuma" is translated by our English words "spirit" or "ghost" as in Holy Spirit or Holy Ghost).

Mormonism and the Holy Spirit and Holy Ghost

"The Holy Ghost should not be confused with the Spirit which fills the immensity of space and which is everywhere present" (Joseph Fielding Smith, *Doctrines of Salvation*, 1:50).

"There are three God's we worship, but an infinite number of Gods" (Bruce McConkie, *Mormon Doctrine*, 322, 576–77).

"The Holy Ghost . . . can be in only one place at one time, and he does not and cannot transform himself into any other form or image other than that of the Man whom he is . . . the Holy Spirit is a Spirit Personage . . . he has power to perform unique functions for men" (Bruce McConkie, *Mormon Doctrine*, 359).

Man and Sin

The Bible: Man and Sin

"The first ploy of Satan in the garden was, "eat of this fruit and you will become like God" (Genesis 3:5).

Mormonism: Man and Sin

"I never speak of the part Eve took in this fall as a sin, nor do I accuse Adam of a sin. It is true, the Lord warned Adam and Eve that to partake of the fruit they would transgress a law, and this happened. But it is not always a sin to transgress a law . . . That is, his transgression was in accordance with law" (Joseph F. Smith, *Doctrines of Salvation*, 1:114).

Salvation

The Bible and Salvation

Ephesians 2:8–9; Acts 4:12; Titus 3:3–7; John 5:24; 2 Corinthians 11:3.

Mormonism and Salvation

"The term salvation is used in two ways. In its general sense, salvation will be given to all men because Christ broke the bands of death . . . Salvation is also used in the Church to mean exaltation" (*Principles of the Gospel*, 276).

"Universal salvation is from physical death, a salvation available to all . . . Individual salvation is another matter . . . there are certain things that must be done in order for divine grace and mercy to be activated" (Robert Millet, *A Different Jesus?*, 81).

"For we know that it is by grace that we are saved, after all we can do" (2 Nephi 25:23, Book of Mormon).

The Bible

Bible References

2 Timothy 3:16; 2 Peter 1:20–21; I Peter 1:23; Proverbs 30:5; John 10:35; Galatians 1:11–12.

The Bible in Mormonism

"The Bible contains the word and will of the Lord to men and women in earlier ages . . . But we do not derive authority to speak or act in the name of Deity on the basis of what God gave to his people in an earlier day" (Robert Millet, *A Different Jesus*, 78).

"The canon of scripture is not full . . . Modern revelation is necessary . . . We must and do believe that he continues to speak" (*Gospel Doctrine*, 36).

"The Bible, in its original form, 'contained the plainness of the gospel of the Lord.' After it had passed through the hands of a 'great and abominable church which is most abominable above all other churches,' however, he saw that 'many plain and precious things' were deleted, in consequence of which error and falsehood poured into the various churches" (1 Nephi 13, Book of Mormon).

APPENDIX D

Correcting the Misuse of Scripture

WHEN MORMON missionaries appear at the door, they will do so with Scriptures in hand, but their first reference will not come from the Book of Mormon—it will likely reference the Holy Bible. Missionaries are trained to use the Bible to "prove" that all other churches are false and to reveal that the LDS Church is the restoration of Christ's church today. These missionaries (and other adherents of Mormonism), take biblical passages out of context or misapply Scripture in an attempt to lend support to their faith. The following scriptural references are some of the most frequently misused texts by the LDS community. The brief responses recorded here are not meant to be exhaustive or all-inclusive, but to give direction to anyone dealing with Mormons to help correct the misuse of these Scriptures.[1]

Old Testament Passages

GENESIS 1:26

Mormonism argues that the use of the word "us" suggests a plurality of Gods. In addition, it is suggested that the Hebrew word translated God, *"Elohim,"* is in the plural and gives credence to the Mormon view of many gods. One should point out that the corresponding Greek noun for God is *"Theos,"* and is always singular.

---

1. For further study, see Reed and Farkas' work, *Mormons Answered Verse by Verse*, or *Correcting the Cults*, by Geisler and Rhodes.

For a person to develop a proper theology, they must deal with this apparent contradiction. How does one reconcile these seemingly contradictory facts? A trip to any Hebrew primer will reveal that the plural Hebrew word for God does not indicate that there is more than one God, but is a frequently used method of expression in Hebrew called the "majestic plural," which gives fullness and speaks of greatness. It does not necessarily represent the plurality of God, but the majesty of God. Grammatically, the "us" in Genesis 1:26 merely reflects the plural form of *Elohim* used in that verse and again, is in keeping with Hebrew grammar.

GENESIS 1:26–27

The argument is often made that since man was formed in God's image, God must possess a physical body. A fundamental hermeneutical principle, however, states that Scripture should interpret Scripture. When other passages about God's nature are consulted, the Mormon understanding of God becomes impossible. John 4:24 indicates that God is spirit. Luke 24:39 tells us that a spirit does not have flesh and bone. Also, the principle of God's omnipresence makes a physical body impossible. Therefore, one must conclude that being made in God's image does not reference man's physical body.

EXODUS 33:11

This verse is often cited by Mormons to prove that God the Father is a man who has achieved godhood and who still has a human-like body. The context shows otherwise. God spoke to Moses from within the pillar of cloud, which served as a visible reminder of his presence. This repeated the pattern of Moses' first conversation with God at the burning bush when he spoke from the midst of a burning bush (Exodus 3:4). There was not a man in the cloud, nor did God hide inside the bush as a man. The point is not that Moses saw a literal face, but that he had a two-way, give-and-take conversation with God. Actually, the context states plainly that Moses did not see God's face. "You cannot see my face, for no one may see me and live" (3:20). God allowed Moses to see his back. Notice God's "hand" shielded Moses. But a man's literal hand would be nowhere near large enough to cover Moses and afford him this protection. Nor could a man's hand remain in place while he passed by. These facts indicate that the references to face, hand, back, are figurative language. The Bible tells us that "No man hath seen God at any time" (Jn 1:18) and that God is a Spirit (Jn 4:24).

DEUTERONOMY 6:4

This passage is used by Mormons to deny the Christian position of the Trinity. Rather than denying the doctrine of the Trinity, this passage actually establishes the fact that there is but one God. To explain this concept, it is necessary to point out that each of the three persons of the Trinity is called God in Scripture. There are three distinct persons within the God-head, but there is only one God (2 Corinthians 13:14 and Matthew 28:19).

1 KINGS 11:1

The LDS view of polygamy is often substantiated by this verse. However, Scripture repeatedly warns against having multiple wives (Deuteronomy 17:17) and violating the principle of monogamy (1 Corinthians 7:2). Polygamy was never established by God for anyone under any circumstance. Polygamy, in Scripture, is mentioned in the context of a sinful society (Genesis 4:19, 23) and every polygamist in the Bible paid dearly for the sin of polygamy. The fact that the Bible records Solomon's (and others) sin of polygamy does not mean that God condoned it.

PSALM 82:6

This verse is used to suggest that man can become a god. Unlike the word LORD (*Yahweh*) which always means God, the words "gods" can be used of: God (Genesis 1:1); angels (Psalms 8:4–6); or even human beings (Psalms 82:6). The author of this Psalm

(Asaph) argues that even though judges were referred to as "gods," they would die like the men they really were (see v. 7).

PSALM 97:7

Mormons suggest that this verse implies many gods, yet the Bible insists there is only one God. To understand this passage, we must realize that there is only one true God, but there are many false gods. Paul declares that there are demons behind false gods (1 Corinthians 10:20) and one day even the demons will bow before the true and living God and confess that he is Lord (Philippians 2:10).

ISAIAH 29:1–4

Mormons suggest that the Book of Mormon is here pictured as being discovered on American soil and that the Nephites are referenced by this passage. The phrase "from the ground" supposedly references the golden plates found by Joseph Smith. But this passage has nothing to do with the so-called Nephites, but with God's judgment against the rebellious Israelites. Jerusalem is called "Ariel" (see Isaiah 29:1; 2 Samuel 5:6–9), which literally means "hearth of God." God's judgment would be so horrific that it would make the city of Jerusalem seem like an altar on which sacrifices were consumed. This judgment found its fulfillment in Sennacherib's siege of the city of Jerusalem in 701 B.C.

JEREMIAH 1:5

Rather than referring to preexistent spirit-children, this passage refers to the prenatal person in the womb. The Hebrew word for "know" (*yada*) implies a special relationship of commitment such as sanctified or ordained. This verse affirms Jeremiah's selection to a special ministry, not to an eternal, preexistent state of man. The Bible does not teach that man's spirit pre-existed but that God formed the spirit of man within him (Zech 12:1).

EZEKIEL 37:16–17

Mormon's believe the "sticks" mentioned in this passage are pieces of wood around which papyrus scrolls were wrapped. One of the sticks (Judah) refers to the Bible; the other (Joseph) allegedly refers to the Book of Mormon. The sticks, however, are not two books, but two kingdoms. The Southern Kingdom was called Judah; the Northern Kingdom was called Israel. The uniting of the "sticks" pictures God's restoring his people into a single nation again (Ezekiel 37:18–28).

MALACHI 3:6

Mormon's argue that because God does not change, he will always communicate with people through new revelation and Scripture. Because God once gave Scripture through prophets, he must always give Scripture through prophets. Consult the immediate context of this passage and it is evident that God is unchanging in his nature, in his purposes, and promises to his people. This verse, however, has nothing to do with the issue of continuing revelation. Other scriptural passages do address the issue of continuing revelation (Jude 3; Galatians 1:8; Acts 17:11; 2 Timothy 3:16).

MALACHI 4:5–6

While it is suggested that this passage predicts the LDS practice of baptism for the dead, this text is a prediction of the coming of "Elijah" before the "great and terrible day of the Lord." John the Baptist becomes the fulfillment of this prophecy.

New Testament Passages

MATTHEW 3:16–17

This passage does not support Mormon polytheism, but a crucial premise of Trinitarianism; that there are three distinct persons of the Godhead. Scripture taken as a whole presents three lines of biblical evidence that need to be considered: (1) there is only one God (Deuteronomy 6:4; 32:39; 2 Samuel 7:22; Psalms 86:10; Isaiah 44:6; John 5:44; 17:3; Romans 3:29–30; 16:27; 1 Corinthians 8:4; Galatians 3:20; Ephesians 4:6; 1 Thessalonians 1:9; 1 Timothy 1:17; 2:5; James 2:19; 1 John 5:20–21; Jude 25); (2) there are three persons who are recognized as God (1 Peter 1:2; John 20:28; Hebrews 1:8; Acts 5:3–4); and, (3) there is a "three-in-oneness" within the God-head (Matthew 28:19; 2 Corinthians 13:14).

Matthew 15:24

Mormons believe the phrase "lost sheep of the house of Israel" refers to Israelites who migrated to America. The context shows, however, that Jesus was referring to Israelites that were spiritually lost, not geographically lost. Jesus' instructions were fulfilled by the preaching of the disciples in and around Palestine, not by preaching in America.

John 2:1–11

Mormons believe that wedding described here is actually the wedding of Jesus. They believe that Jesus was married at Cana. A simple look at the context reveals that Jesus is a guest not a participant. His comment, "Woman what does this have to do with me?" shows that he is uninvolved. Jesus also leaves this wedding with his disciples and his mother.

1 Corinthians 15:29

Rather than supporting a doctrine that living believers should be baptized on behalf of those who are dead, Paul rhetorically asks, "If you don't believe in the resurrection of the dead, then why are new converts (who one day will die) baptized?"

1 Corinthians 15:40–42

The context of this passage does not support the LDS view that all people will inhabit one of three kingdoms of glory. Paul in these verses contrasts heavenly (celestial) bodies with earthly (terrestrial) bodies. He relates that the earthly body is fallen, temporal, imperfect and weak, while the heavenly body will be eternal and perfect. The contrast is between heavenly bodies and earthly bodies and does not describe kingdoms of glory.

2 Corinthians 12:2

While three heavens are mentioned here, and commonly spoken about in Greek literature, these are not the Celestial, Terrestrial and Telestial Kingdoms of Mormonism. Scripture reveals that the three heavens include: the atmospheric heaven (Deuteronomy 11:11); the starry heaven (Genesis 1:14); and the heaven where God dwells (Isaiah 63:15). Paul here refers to this third heaven.

2 Thessalonians 2:3; 1 Timothy 4:1, 2

Mormons use these verses to suggest that the church totally disappeared from the face of the earth and was not restored until Joseph Smith did so in the early 1800's. These passages, however, do not say that Christianity would disappear or that all would fall away, but that some might depart from the faith.

James 1:5

Mormons appeal to this verse in asking people to pray to see if the Book of Mormon is true. The meaning of this verse must be connected with the preceding verses about the purpose of trials. Prayer is not the test for religious truth. 1 Thessalonians 5:21 teaches us to "test all things," not to rely on a subjective feeling for authenticity based on prayer.

APPENDIX E

Conversations to Avoid

As you lovingly witness with your Mormon friends, it is easy to offend someone when a truth is presented that conflicts with their belief system. While it is impossible to correct error without risking the possibility of offending, some topics are more offensive and less effective than others. It is recommended that you avoid these types of topics in your initial discussions with Mormons. The point is not to avoid all offensive material, but rather to avoid needlessly offending someone with nonessential, side issues. The following topics are likely to result in conflict and debate which are not only unnecessary, but ineffective in winning Mormons to Christ. It is recommended that you initially steer clear of these topics:

- The Adam-God doctrine
- Baptism for the dead
- Mocking of Mormon prophets
- The Mountain Meadow Massacre
- The no-coffee restrictions
- Polygamy
- Secret and sacred temple rites
- Temple garments and holy underwear

Eventually, it may become necessary to discuss some or all of these topics with your Mormon friends, but first focus on more important topics, such as the biblical doctrines of God, salvation, and the trustworthiness of the Bible.

Also, avoid personal attacks at all costs. You will be more successful as you witness to Mormons if you avoid personal pronouns. For example, don't say, "You are not a Christian." Instead say, "Mormonism is not Christian." Don't say, "You believe [this or that]." Instead ask, "Doesn't the Mormon Church teach [this or that]?" By leaving out personal pronouns, your hearers will not be as prone to think that you are attacking them personally.

APPENDIX F

Other Discussions with Your Mormon Friends

Families Are Forever

ONE OF the greatest drawing cards of the Mormon Church is their emphasis on families. A simple comment about your appreciation for the closeness of Mormon families and the emphasis of the Mormon Church on the family unit will likely lead your Mormon friend directly to this topic. They will typically ask of you, "Don't you want to have your wife/husband and children with you forever?" This doctrine comes from Joseph Smith, as recorded in The Doctrine and Covenants sections 131 and 132. In Mormonism, husbands and wives are sealed together in the temple for time and eternity, and children are also sealed eternally to parents. But there is a problem reconciling this doctrine with other Mormon teachings. For example, the goal of every Mormon is to be "exalted to godhood." If exaltation is achieved, a man will literally become a god of his own world. If this is true, how can families be together for all eternity? Instead of being together, won't the best Mormon families literally be worlds apart on different planets?

Mormons have no reasonable explanation. When confronted with this dilemma, you can expect to hear, "We don't understand everything, but God will work it all out." This is your opportunity to share with them what Jesus said about marriage in heaven.

That same day the Sadducees, who say there is no resurrection, came to him with a question. "Teacher," they said, "Moses told us that if a man dies without having children, his brother must marry the widow and have children for him. Now there were seven brothers among us. The first one married and died, and since he had no children, he left his wife to his brother. The same thing happened to the second and third brother, right down to the seventh. Finally, the woman died. Now then, at the resurrection, whose wife will she be of the seven, since all of them were married to her?" Jesus replied, "You are in error because you do not know the Scriptures or the power of God. At the resurrection people will neither marry nor be given in marriage; they will be like the angels in heaven." (Matthew 22:23–30)

Trusting Your Heart

The Mormon Church encourages its people to trust their hearts.[1] When they give you a Book of Mormon they will ask you to pray about it and seek a "burning in your bosom." If you bring into question a Mormon doctrine, they will often respond, "But my heart tells me that the Book of Mormon and the Mormon Church are true." You should use this as an opportunity to share with your Mormon friend what the Bible says about trusting your heart. "The heart is deceitful above all things and beyond cure. Who can understand it?" (Jeremiah 17:9). Jesus said, "What comes out of a man is what makes him 'unclean.' For from within, out of men's hearts, come evil thoughts, sexual immorality, theft, murder, adultery, greed, malice, deceit, lewdness, envy, slander, arrogance and

---

1. John Widtsoe writes, "Thousands have tried this approach to truth; and have found the testimonies they sought. So far, no one who, with flaming desire, sincere prayer, earnest study, and fearless practice, has sought the truth of 'Mormonism' has failed to find it. Some, for lack of courage, though truth stared them in the face, have kept it to themselves. But, the approach never fails, so declares fearlessly the Church of Jesus Christ of Latter-day Saints" (*Evidences and Reconciliations*, 17).

folly. All these evils come from inside and make a man 'unclean'" (Mark 7:20–23).

One God or Three

As you talk about God, the issue of the Trinity will immediately present itself. The Bible teaches that God is a three-in-one, triune being. To reconcile their belief, Mormons will try to convince you that there is only one God of this earth and only one God that they worship. You can respond in one of two ways. First, ask your Mormon friend to show you one place in the Bible or The Book of Mormon where it says there is more than one true God. They will not be able to do so. Second, ask them which Mormon God they worship: God the Father, God the Son, or God the Holy Spirit. Ask them specifically, "Doesn't Mormonism teach that they are all gods of this earth? Doesn't Mormonism worship all three of these Gods?"

The Virgin Birth

The Mormon doctrine of a Godhead composed of three separate Gods forces Mormonism to reject the thought that the Holy Spirit was involved in the Virgin Birth. If this was true, Jesus would have to be called the "Son of the Holy Ghost" instead of the "Son of God the Father." Mormonism teaches that God the Father had a physical relationship with Mary, and she conceived Jesus in the same natural way that all children are conceived on this earth. This doctrine destroys the teaching that Christ was born of a virgin.

APPENDIX G

How to Remove Your Name
from Mormon Records

UNLESS AN exiting Mormon officially asks to be removed from the records, the Church of Jesus Christ of Latter-Day Saints will carry their name indefinitely—even if that person has not attended in years. This highly questionable practice of claiming inactive people as members not only artificially skews the numbers that the church uses for publicity, but creates a false sense of excitement regarding church growth and is used by them as a means of validating the claims of Mormonism. By resigning membership, an exiting member delivers an important message that the leadership needs to hear: "I am not a Mormon, and something is seriously wrong with Mormonism."

More importantly, when a person asks to be removed from the records of the Mormon church, an important psychological (maybe even spiritual) connection is broken. Many people feel a very real emotional release after verbally renouncing, then formally resigning from the Mormon Church.

Resigning can be accomplished by mail, but letters must be sent to three people. Make sure that each copy lists all those receiving copies. It is unnecessary to attend an "excommunication court," even if requested to do so. Send letters to the following three people:

1. The Bishop of the Mormon Ward where you currently reside.
2. The Stake President.

3. The President of the Mormon Church (The President can be reached by mailing the letter to the following address: The Church Office Building, Salt Lake City, UT).

The resignation letter should be polite, but firm. It should be in your own words. Here is a sample letter:

Dear Bishop, Stake President, and President:

This letter is to inform you that I wish to resign membership and request that my name be removed from all records of the Church of Jesus Christ of Latter-day Saints.

I have made this decision of my own free will and have not been coerced or pressured in any way. I insist that the Church record show the only reason for my termination of membership is this request. Please notify me by letter when this has been accomplished. I will not hesitate to take immediate legal action if anything is done to libel my name or cause me any loss of reputation. I further insist that you honor my request in a timely manner. Copies of this letter have been sent to all those addressed above.

I have many doctrinal differences with the Mormon Church: I do not believe that Joseph Smith was a prophet; I do not believe the Book of Mormon is the Word of God; nor do I believe that the Mormon Church has restored the gospel of Jesus Christ.

I have come to this decision after much prayer and my decision is absolutely final. Any attempt to contact me by any Missionary or other representative of the LDS Church will be considered to be an invasion of my privacy. Since I have done nothing wrong, I will not participate in a Church trial or court hearing.

Thank you for your attention in this matter and honoring my request.

Sincerely, (Signature)

APPENDIX H

LDS Leaders—Past and Present

THE FOLLOWING is an alphabetical listing of many LDS Church leaders who have been quoted throughout this book. Each man's position has been included to substantiate that the sources quoted are not from those on the fringe of Mormonism, but serve in the Church's top positions. The President of the church, commonly referred to as the Prophet, holds the top position in the LDS Church. He and two counselors make up the First Presidency. Next in line are the Twelve Apostles of the First Quorum of the Seventy, followed by the Second Quorum of the Seventy. Three other individuals are authors and current professors at Brigham Young University.

Benson, Ezra Taft (1899–1994) Thirteenth President
Cowdery, Oliver (1806–1850) Assistant President under Joseph Smith
Grant, Heber J. (1856–1945) Seventh President
Hinckley, Gordon B. (1910–2008) Fifteenth President
Holland, Jeffrey R. (1940–) Apostle
Hunter, Howard W. (1907–1995) Fourteenth President
Hunter, Milton R. (1902–1975) First Council of the Seventy
Hyde, Orson (1805–1878) Apostle
Kimball, Heber C. (1801–1868) First Counselor in the First Presidency
Kimball, Spencer W. (1895–1985) Twelfth President
Lee, Harold B. (1899–1973) Eleventh President
McConkie, Bruce R. (1915–1985) Apostle

McKay, David O. (1873–1970) Ninth President

Millet, Robert L. (1947–) Professor of Religious Understanding at BYU

Monson, Thomas (1927–) Sixteenth President

Packer, Boyd K. (1924–) Apostle

Pratt, Orson (1811–1881) Apostle

Pratt, Parley P. (1807–1857) Apostle

Richards, LeGrand (1886–1983) Apostle

Rigdon, Sidney (1793–1876) First Counselor in the First Presidency

Roberts, B. H. (1857–1933) Seventy

Robinson, Stephen E. (1947–) Professor at BYU

Smith, George A. (1870–1951) Eight President

Smith, Hyrum (1800–1844) Assistant President under Joseph Smith

Smith, Joseph, Jr. (1805–1844) First President and founder

Smith, Joseph F. (1838–1918) Sixth President

Smith, Joseph Fielding (1876–1972) Tenth President

Snow, Lorenzo (1814–1901) Fifth President

Talmage, James E. (1862–1933) Apostle

Taylor, John (1808–1887) Third President

Widtsoe, John A. (1872–1952) Apostle

Williams, Drew (1954–) Professor at BYU

Woodruff, Wilford (1807–1898) Fourth President

Young, Brigham (1801–1877) Second President

Bibliography

LDS Sources

Achieving a Celestial Marriage. Salt Lake City, Utah: Church of Jesus Christ of Latter-day Saints, 1992.

Benson, Ezra Taft. *The Teachings of Ezra Taft Benson*. Salt Lake City, Utah: Bookcraft, 1988.

Blomberg, Craig L., and Stephen E. Robinson. *How Wide the Divide? A Mormon and an Evangelical in Conversation*. Downers Grove, Illinois: InterVarsity Press, 1997.

Conference Report of the Church of Jesus Christ of Latter-day Saints. April 1907 through April 2004.

Ensign. Select issues from the magazine, published monthly by the LDS Church since 1971. Salt Lake City: The Church of Jesus Christ of Latter-day Saints.

Family Home Evening Manual. Salt Lake City: The Church of Jesus Christ of Latter-day Saints, 1972.

Gospel Principles. Salt Lake City, Utah: Church of Jesus Christ of Latter-day Saints, 1981.

Hinckley, Gordon B. *Be Thou An Example*. Salt Lake City, Utah: Deseret Book, 1981.

———. *Teachings of Gordon B. Hinckley*. Salt Lake City, Utah: Deseret Book, 1997.

History of the Church of Jesus Christ of Latter-day Saints, 7 vols. Edited by B. H. Roberts. Salt Lake City, Utah: Deseret Book, 1957.

Hunter, Milton R. *Gospel Through the Ages*. Salt Lake City, Utah: Deseret Book Co., 1958.

Journal of Discourses. 26 vols. Liverpool: F.D. Richards & Sons, 1851–86.

Kimball, Edward, ed. *The Teachings of Spencer W. Kimball*. Salt Lake City, Utah: Bookcraft, 1982.

Kimball, Spencer W. *The Miracle of Forgiveness*. Salt Lake City, Utah: Bookcraft, 1969.

————. *Repentance Brings Forgiveness*. Salt Lake City, Utah: The Church of Jesus Christ of Latter-day Saints, 1984.

Ludlow, Daniel H., ed. *Encyclopedia of Mormonism*. 4 vols. New York: Macmillan, 1992.

McConkie, Bruce R. *Doctrinal New Testament Commentary*, Salt Lake City, Utah: Bookcraft, 1976.

————. *Mormon Doctrine*. 2nd ed. Salt Lake City, Utah: Bookcraft, 1977.

————. *A New Witness for the Articles of Faith*. Salt Lake City, Utah: Deseret Book Co., 1985.

————. *The Promised Messiah*. Salt Lake City, Utah: Deseret Book, 1978.

McKay, David O. *Gospel Ideals*. Salt Lake City: The Improvement Era, 1953.

Millet, Robert L. *A Different Jesus? The Christ of the Latter-day Saints*. Grand Rapids: Eerdmans, 2005.

————. *The Mormon Faith: A New Look at Christianity*. Salt Lake City: Deseret Book Co., 1998.

Millet, Robert and Greg Johnson. *A Mormon & Evangelical Christian in Conversation: Truth Matters, People Matter, Relationships Matter, Lunch Matters*. Boise, Idaho: Search Ministries, March, 2004.

————. *A Mormon & Evangelical Christian in Conversation: A Conversation on The First Vision of Joseph Smith*. Boise, Idaho: Search Ministries, March 4, 2005.

————. *A Mormon & Evangelical Christian in Conversation: The Nature of Jesus Christ*. Boise, Idaho: Search Ministries, February 15, 2006.

Pratt, Orson. *Orson Pratt's Works*. Salt Lake City: Deseret News Press, 1945.

————. *The Seer*. Washington, D.C.: N.P., 1853–54.

Richards, F. D., comp. *Journal of Discourses*. 26 vols. Liverpool: Latter-day Saint Book Depot, 1855–1886.

Richards, LeGrand. *A Marvelous Work and a Wonder*. Salt Lake City, Utah: Deseret Book Co., 1976.

Roberts, B. H. *New Witnesses for God*. Vol. 1, in *LDS Collector's Library*, CD-ROM, 1997.

Robinson, Stephen E. *Believing Christ*. Provo, Utah: Deseret, 1992.

————. *Are Mormons Christians?* Salt Lake City, Utah: Bookcraft, 1991.

Smith, Joseph Jr. The Book of Mormon. Palmyra, N.Y.: Grandin, 1830; Rev. ed., Salt Lake City, Utah: Corporation of the Church of Jesus Christ of Latter-day Saints, 1981.

————. The Doctrine and Covenants. Kirtland, Ohio: 1835; Rev. ed., Salt Lake City, Utah: Corporation of the Church of Jesus Christ of Latter-day Saints, 1981.

————. *Documented History of the Church of Jesus Christ of Latter-day Saints*. 6 vols. edited by B. H. Roberts. Salt Lake City, Utah: Deseret Book Co., 1978.

———. Pearl of Great Price. Liverpool: 1851; Rev. ed., Salt Lake City, Utah: Corporation of the Church of Jesus Christ of Latter-day Saints, 1981.

———. *Teachings of the Prophet Joseph Smith*. Selected by Joseph Fielding Smith. Salt Lake City, Utah: Deseret Book, 1976.

———. *The Words of Joseph Smith*. Edited by Andrew F. Ehat and Lyndon W. Cook. Provo: BYU Religious Studies Center, 1980.

Smith, Joseph Fielding. *Doctrines of Salvation*. 3 vols. Salt Lake City, Utah: Bookcraft, 1959.

———. *Essentials in Church History*. Salt Lake City, Utah: Deseret News Press, 1942.

———. *The Way to Perfection*. Salt Lake City, Utah: Genealogical Society of Utah, 1931.

Snow, Lorenzo. *The Teachings of Lorenzo Snow*. Edited by Clyde J. Williams. Salt Lake City, Utah: Bookcraft, 1984.

Statement of the First Presidency of The Church of Jesus Christ of Latter-day Saints, 15 February 1978.

Talmage, James E. *Articles of Faith*. Salt Lake City, Utah: Deseret Book Co., 1981.

———. *The Great Apostasy*. Salt Lake City, Utah: Deseret Book Company, 1975.

Taylor, John. *The Gospel Kingdom*. Salt Lake City, Utah: Bookcraft, 1964.

Teachings of Presidents of the Church—Brigham Young. Salt Lake City, Utah: The Church of Jesus Christ of Latter-day Saints, 1998.

Teachings of Presidents of the Church—Joseph Smith. Salt Lake City, Utah: The Church of Jesus Christ of Latter-day Saints, 1998.

Teachings of the Living Prophets. Salt Lake City, Utah: The Church of Jesus Christ of Latter-day Saints, 1982.

Times and Seasons. A six-volume series that contains copies of the LDS newspaper printed between November 1839 and February 15, 1846.

Uniform System for Teaching the Gospel. Salt Lake City, Utah: Corporation of the President of the Church of Jesus Christ of Latter-day Saints, 1986.

Whitmer, David. *An Address to All Believers in Christ*. Richmond, Missouri: David Whitmer, 1887.

Widtsoe, John A. *Evidences and Reconciliations*. Salt Lake City, Utah: Bookcraft, 1987.

———. *Joseph Smith—Seeker After Truth*. Salt Lake City, Utah: Deseret, 1951.

———. *Priesthood and Church Government*. Salt Lake City, Utah: Deseret Book Company, 1967.

Williams, Drew. *Understanding Mormonism*. New York: Penguin Group, 2003.

Woodruff, Wilford. *The Discourses of Wilford Woodruff*. Selected by G. Homer Durham. Salt Lake City, Utah: Bookcraft, 1946.

Non-LDS Sources

Ankerberg, John, and John Weldon. *Everything You Ever Wanted to Know about Mormonism.* Eugene, OR: Harvest House, 1992.

Beckwith, Francis J. "Philosophical Problems with the Mormon Concept of God," *Christian Research Journal,* Spring 1992, p. 28.

Beckwith, Francis J., Carl Mosser and Paul Owen. *The New Mormon Challenge: Responding to the Latest Defenses of a Fast-Growing Movement.* Grand Rapids: Zondervan, 2002.

Blomberg, Craig L., and Stephen E. Robinson. *How Wide the Divide? A Mormon and an Evangelical in Conversation.* Downers Grove, Illinois: InterVarsity Press, 1997.

Cares, Mark J. *Speaking the Truth in Love to Mormons.* Milwaukee, WI: Northwestern Publishing House, 1993.

Crane, Charles. *The Bible and Mormon Scriptures Compared.* Joplin, MO: College Press, 1992.

———. *Christianity and Mormonism, From Bondage to Freedom.* Webb City: MO: Covenant Publishing, 2002.

Crane, Charles and Steven. *Ashamed of Joseph: Mormon Foundations Crumble.* Joplin, MO: College Press, 1993.

Fraser, Gordon H. *Is Mormonism Christian?* Chicago: Moody, 1977.

———. *Joseph and the Golden Plates.* Eugene, OR: Industrial Litho, Inc., 1978.

———. *What Does the Book of Mormon Teach?* Chicago: Moody, 1964.

Geisler, Norman L., and Ron Rhodes. *Correcting the Cults: Expert Responses to Their Scripture Twisting.* Grand Rapids: Baker, 1997.

———. *When Cultists Ask: A Popular Handbook on Cultic Misinterpretations.* Grand Rapids: Baker, 1997.

Lucado, Max. *A Gentle Thunder: Hearing God Through the Storm.* Dallas: Word Publishing, 1995.

McKeever, Bill. *Answering Mormon's Questions.* Minneapolis, Minnesota: Bethany House, 1991.

McKeever, Bill and Eric Johnson. *Questions to Ask Your Mormon Friend: Challenging the Claims of Latter-day Saints in a Constructive Manner.* Minneapolis, Minnesota: Bethany House, 1994.

Martin, Walter. *The New Cults.* Ventura, California: Regal Books, 1980.

Millet, Robert and Greg Johnson, *A Mormon & Evangelical Christian in Conversation: Truth Matters, People Matter, Relationships Matter, Lunch Matters.* Boise, Idaho: Search Ministries, March, 2004.

———. *A Mormon & Evangelical Christian in Conversation: A Conversation on The First Vision of Joseph Smith.* Boise, Idaho: Search Ministries, March 4, 2005.

————. *A Mormon & Evangelical Christian in Conversation: The Nature of Jesus Christ.* Boise, Idaho: Search Ministries, February 15, 2006.

Reed, David A. and John R. Farkas. *Mormons Answered Verse by Verse.* Grand Rapids, Michigan: Baker Book House, 1992.

Rhodes, Ron and Marian Bodine. *Reasoning from the Scriptures with the Mormons.* Eugene, OR: Harvest House Publishers, 1995.

Roberts, R. Philip. *Mormonism Unmasked.* Nashville: Broadman and Holman Publishers, 1998.

Ropp, Harry L. *Is Mormonism Christian? A Look at the Teachings of the Mormon Religion.* Revised by Charles A. Crane. Joplin, MI: College Press, 1995.

Rowe, David L. *I Love Mormons: A New Way to Share Christ with Latter-day Saints.* Grand Rapids: Baker Books, 2005.

Scott, Latayne C. *After Mormonism, What?* Grand Rapids: Baker Books, 1994.

Spencer, James R. *Beyond Mormonism: An Elder's Story.* Boise, ID: Through the Maze, 2005.

Spry, Jeff A. *The Preparation and Delivery of Expository Doctrinal Sermons.* D.Min thesis project, Gordon-Conwell Theological Seminary, 2007.

Tanner, Jerald and Sandra. *3913 Changes in the Book of Mormon.* Salt Lake City, UT: Utah Lighthouse Ministry, N.D.

————. *Archaeology and the Book of Mormon.* Salt Lake City, UT: Modern Microfilm Company, 1989.

————. *The Changing World of Mormonism.* Chicago, IL: Moody Press, 1981.

————. *Major Problems of Mormonism.* Salt Lake City, UT: Utah Lighthouse Ministry, 1989.

————. *Mormonism—Shadow or Reality?* 4th edition. Salt Lake City, Utah: Modern Microfilm Company, 1979.

About the Author

D R. S TEVEN A. Crane graduated from Puget Sound Christian College in 1987 with a Bachelor of Arts in Preaching. In 1990, he received a Master of Arts in Practical Ministry from Pacific Christian College. In 1995, he received a Master of Divinity in Theology from Lincoln Christian Seminary. In 2007, he received his Doctor of Ministry from Gordon-Conwell Theological Seminary.

In 1995, Steve planted Eagle Christian Church (ECC) with the belief that Eagle was "under-churched" and needed a "non-denominational," Bible-believing church. From a humble beginning with just seven people, ECC has grown in its weekend attendance to a church of 2,200. In addition to his ministry at ECC, he teaches part-time at Boise Bible College (BBC). He has served at BBC since 1990.

Steve is married with four children and is the co-Author of *Ashamed of Joseph: Mormon Foundations Crumble.*